**Experienced travelers know
it pays to learn the rules of the road**

"Read it before you leave home, and you may get where you're going in better spirits."
—*The Robb Report*

"The book discusses the seldom explained rights of airline passengers, car rental clients, credit car holders, and other travel industry 'secrets' every traveler should learn."
—*AAA Motorland*

"Mr. Leocha also unmasks such confusing areas as credit cards ... taxes ... and complaints. He lists addresses and contacts for travel-related consumer protection agencies and airline, rental car and credit card customer service departments."
—*The National Law Journal*

"*Travel Rights* prepares travelers, by fastening their seat belts for the unfortunate, though not unforeseen, bumpy ride that awaits them."
—*Travel Weekly*

"*Travel Rights* can be whipped out for guidance if you need to know how to file claims for lost luggage ... when to rely on credit-card rental-car collision insurance ... or how to recover overseas sales taxes."
—*Inc. Magazine*

"You can't always avoid travel hassles, but you can get out of plenty of sticky situations with a little help from *Travel Rights*."
—*Entrepreneur*

"*Travel Rights* helps you become a savvy traveler who knows your rights."
—*Affordable Travel*

About the author

Charlie Leocha has been traveling since the age of two when his family moved from Alabama to Virginia. He is an Air Force brat who spent half his life abroad. He had the measles crossing the Atlantic on a troop ship, started school in Naples wearing a smock and bow, sang *If I Had a Hammer* on Red Square in '68, criss-crossed Europe in a camper van, skied at every major resort in America and the Alps, did basic training in the fields of Kansas, rafted in Costa Rica, walked through the rubble of the Berlin Wall, horsebacked through Utah, caroused with flight attendants, and still runs the bulls in Pamplona religiously. He has been stuck in most major U.S. airports, been bumped from scores of flights, and found many ways to be upgraded.

Charlie started a leisure magazine in Europe for Americans living abroad. His *Travel Tips* radio program has been heard on hundreds of stations and he has appeared on TV across the country. He is the creator of the *Escape Manual Travel Guides, Skiing America, Ski Europe,* and *Eastern Germany.* He has written about travel for scores of newspapers, and magazines ranging from *Esquire, Newsweek* and *Travel and Leisure,* to the top magazines that serve the travel industry. He knows major airlines from the inside, has led tour groups, written vacation brochures, produced travel videos and written speeches for airline presidents.

Disclaimers Use this book only as a guide

It is not out intent to provide legal advice. We make no guarantee as to the validity or applicability of this information. Anything we observe in this book, except federal and international regulations, can be changed without notice, and often is. Nothing is carved in stone— especially when dealing with the travel industry.

Most situations can be sorted out with common sense— that is the good part about the limited regulation of the travel industry. The company representatives' basic instinct is to keep the customer satisfied, unless you back them into a corner where they may bite back.

TRAVEL RIGHTS

by Charles Leocha

WORLD LEISURE CORP.

P.O. Box 160, Hampstead, NH 03841

Distributed to national chains, Ingram,
Baker & Taylor, Bookazine in USA by
Midwest Trade Books, Inc.
27 W. 20th St., Suite 1102
New York, NY 10011
Tel. (212) 727-0190, fax (212) 727-0195

Distributed to independent bookstores, regional chains,
and other wholesalers by
The Talman Company
89 Fifth Ave., New York, NY 10003
Tel. (800) 537-8894, fax (212) 352-1772

Distributed to the trade in U.K. by
Portfolio, Unit 1c, West Ealing Business Centre,
Alexandria Road, London W13 0NJ
Tel. (0181) 579-7748, fax (0181) 567-0904

Mail Order, Catalog, other International sales and rights,
and Special Sales by
World Leisure Corporation
177 Paris St., Boston, MA 02128
Tel. (617) 569-1966, fax (617) 561-7654

E-mail: wleisure@aol.com; Internet: www.worldleisure.com

ISBN: 0-915009-57-9

G151. L46 1994

Contents

Introduction

This book lets travelers know the way it is and hopefully will help airline passengers, rental car clients and credit card users avoid problems and get the best possible service available with the fewest hassles. This book outlines the basic rules, regulations, and policies that dictate how airlines, automobile rental companies, and credit card issuers work with their customers. This is not a book about "Travel Secrets" or "Insider Tricks."

Travel Rights also delves into the new world of the airline Internet sites. The main airline sites are listed as well as some of the best World Wide Web addresses that can help with making plans for travel.

Almost all seasoned travelers have been faced with travel hassles—being bumped off an airline flight, missing connections because of a late arrival, having baggage lost, or being delayed by weather. Others have been faced with rental car reservations that have disappeared or pondered whether they really needed that collision damage waiver counter personnel present when signing rental contracts. And it is a traveler's nightmare to ever have to deal with losing a passport while traveling abroad.

When everything works well, business and vacation travelers return with smiles on their faces. But, when things go wrong, those smiles can change to frustrated frowns and anger. To make the best of travel gone awry, travelers need to know their Travel Rights so they can get to their destination—on time and with all their belongings—as quickly and easily as possible.

The industry works together

There are thousands of tales of woe and complaints about airline, rental car and credit card companies.

Though the government has stringent laws that regulate safety, there are very few instances where passenger service is covered by federal law.

Airline and car rental companies have developed detailed policies that allow their representatives to help travelers in distress whether caused by simply a delay or by a family emergency.

When it is beyond the means of an airline to conveniently reschedule passengers or deliver delayed baggage, other airlines pitch in and help. Counter and baggage personnel, flight attendants and pilots all know that when their airline is faced with a similar crisis, other airlines will help them as well. The same airlines which compete fiercely in the marketplace with discounts, service and schedules also work together and cooperate with each other to create an unprecedented reciprocal network that can take care of their passengers and customers.

What are Travel Rights?

The more specifics travelers know about this system of inter-airline assistance as well as the complicated airline ticketing options and scores of special passenger services, the better they can take advantage of these options when traveling.

The better rental car customers understand pricing policies, collision damage waiver regulations, driver license checks and additional charges, the easier it becomes for counter personnel to explain special deals and for travelers to clearly compare prices and services.

The more credit card holders learn about the many benefits of "plastic," the more they will realize what a treasure a good credit card can be. Credit card services help with everything from getting prescriptions filled overseas to medical care and everyday blessings like taking money from bank machines in virtually every corner of the world and paying for everything from meals to taxis in many countries.

All of these travel benefits, company policies, as obscure as they may be, together with a couple of federal laws, make up a traveler's Travel Rights. In the following pages—clearly indexed and with a simple table of contents—you will learn about Travel Rights most travelers don't even know they have.

Getting the word out

Airlines, automobile rental companies and credit card issuers all spend small fortunes attempting to let travelers know about all the deals and benefits available to them. But the information is overwhelming and it comes in scores of brochures, with credit card bills, on the back of airline tickets, in fine print on car rental agreements, with coupons in grocery stores, tucked in marketing pitches, and on Internet Web sites.

Honestly, how many of us have ever really read the extra pages in an airline ticket? How many of us have ever taken the time to read the detailed description of credit card benefits every issuing bank sends to credit card holders? Who really knows what they can ask for from a Consulate or Embassy abroad? *Travel Rights* takes that information and makes it easy to find, easy to read and easy to use. When travelers know their Travel Rights, they know what they can expect from the travel industry.

Information overload

This deluge of so much information serves to keep most travelers confused and relatively clueless concerning everyday and extraordinary Travel Rights.

On top of the basic problem of digesting so much information, once the curious traveler has learned the rules of one airline, rental car company or credit card, The next airline, car rental or credit card company may have (and probably does have) significantly different policies. Plus, when it comes to customer service, nothing is carved in stone.

The federal regulation mantra

Flight attendants and airline administrators repeatedly intone the mantra "Federal Regulation." In actuality, *official* regulation barely exists when it comes to customer service. Airline, rental car and credit card company policies are the *real* rules by which the travel industry works. *Travel Rights* clarifies some of these rules. Knowing them can make a big, big difference both when planning a trip and when problems arise during travels.

○ If your plane is delayed several hours by a mechanical problem, what do airline rules allow you?

○ If you are bumped off a flight involuntarily and miss a business meeting, do you get the same treatment as a volunteer bumpee, gleeful at the idea of a free ticket?

○ Are charter flights really different from scheduled airlines, or only a bargain?

○ When planning to travel with friends and family, and you have *multiple drivers* for a rental car, do you know which companies don't charge extra for additional drivers? Is your credit card Collision Damage Waiver still valid for those drivers?

○ What credit cards are best for travel? Do you know their real benefits?

○   Wonder when you have to pay sales taxes and when you don't? Do you know that after you pay some taxes in Europe and in Canada *you can get most of your money back*?

○   Do you *really* know how to replace a passport in a day when traveling abroad?

○   Do you know what travel information can be found on the Internet and what sites allow secure reservation systems?

Today, the Zen of Travel predominates, and reaching your destination is no longer the only goal. The journey there, with some sense of style and comfort, is more important. Though airlines compete based on destination they go to great lengths to provide enhanced services based on factors such as nonstop flights, size of seats, frequency of service, and on-time records. Rental car companies strive to make picking up a rental car as easy as walking to your garage.

Options for travelers are far more extensive than most realize. The bottom line is that travelers need to know what their options may be. I hope this book sheds a bit of light on the world in which we travel and makes it easier to ask knowledgeably for our Travel Rights.

Airline Rights

The airline industry seems, at first glance, to be one of the most regulated sectors of the world economy, with aviation authorities and commissions abounding everywhere on the globe. Air traffic is closely monitored, aircraft are carefully inspected and expertly maintained, routes are approved by bureaucracies, small regional carriers are subsidized, reservation systems are scrutinized, flight records are kept mile by mile, and much more.

Though you seem to hear "due to federal regulation" after every sentence when your flight attendant gives a safety briefing, in the area of passenger service the industry is barely regulated. The Department of Transportation (DOT) has established a bare-bones Code of Federal Regulation and each air carrier designs its own rules to fall within these limits. During the initial research of this book, DOT's Aviation Consumer Protection Division was more helpful and responsive than I believed a government bureaucracy could be. And subsequent reports from travelers faced with problems showed a government agency that works as a very effective advocate for travelers.

The most important manual when it comes to what airlines can or cannot do for passengers is found in an airline's passenger service manual. Every customer service representative studies these pages and the frequent updates; however, you won't find many of the airline personnel turning to these tomes when questioned by passengers. Common sense seems to prevail except in extreme cases.

Passenger service manuals are updated and revised frequently. Most of the information in these manuals can be discovered on a case-by-case basis and passengers can request to see the policies from the airline ticket counter if they have specific questions.

These internal policies are part of each airline's competitive posture within the travel industry. Passenger service is now as important a consideration for most travelers as finding a nonstop flight and securing the lowest airfare. As you use this book, realize that we provide only *guidelines* for your flying rights—every airline has its own domestic and international rules.

To take you through this labyrinth we focus on the following areas:

- **Who sells airline tickets**—travel agents and airlines; the best ways to purchase airline tickets, get refunds, and deal with lost tickets.

- **Contracts of Carriage**—every airline traveler signs this when they purchase a ticket for air travel on scheduled airlines, and we explore the even more consumer-unfriendly details of Public Charters.

- **Understanding the airfare maze**—outlining the various classes of tickets and highlighting some of the discounts available to travelers as well as the rules that accompany these fares.

- **Preflight decisions**—dealing with infants, selecting seats, arranging for wheelchairs or other assistance, and ordering special meals.

- **Dealing with problems enroute**—delayed and canceled flights, lost tickets, overbooking and bumping.

- **Baggage problems**—baggage check-in limits, carry-on limits, lost and delayed bags, damaged bags, and additional insurance.

- **On-board health** considerations and miscellaneous airline considerations.

Purchasing Tickets—
Travel Agents &
Consolidators

Why a travel agent can help

Travel agents sell most of the airline tickets and hotel rooms in America. Hence, a travel agent often has clout and know-how that can make your trip easier and more enjoyable.

More important in most cases than clout, travel agents have access to one of the major central reservation systems. These high-powered systems allow agents to have real-time access to airline seat inventories and the systems provide programs that ferret out the lowest prices available between points for air travelers.

Legally, travel agents contract with airlines to sell passengers airline tickets. Until recently, travel agents have been paid by the airlines to sell you tickets. Keep this in mind when you work through a travel agent—they represent the airlines—they do not represent you.

Recently, with the cutbacks in travel agent commissions, some agencies have begun to assess a small fee to offset their costs. Now that travel agencies are collecting a fee directly from passengers, a new legal relationship is being forged. This relationship has not been tested to date, but the rules of the game are changing. Now that some passengers are paying the agencies, the agency now is working for the passenger, not the airline.

NOTE: All travel agents are not the same. Some specialize in European travel, others are experts in Asian travel, others deal with cruise ships, and yet others provide bargain-basement travel throughout the year. However, the following points apply to all of them:

● Your airfare is the same whether you purchase your tickets directly from the airline or through a travel agent. Though some travel agents have begun to charge minimal fees, the services travel agents provide often more than make up for the small charge. Note below.

● Some travel agents will check fares periodically for you even after a ticket is purchased and alert you to a lower fare and then will change your ticket to save you money. You will never find an airline calling with a lower fare and offering to change your ticket.

● There are no advantages to buying your tickets directly from the airlines. With airfares changing as quickly as they seem to, travel agents provide the easiest way to change tickets in order to get a lower airfare if one should be implemented between the time you purchase your ticket and your flight. Though airlines claim they can reissue your tickets at the new lower rates, you have to go to the airport, or an airline ticket office, which in most cases is less convenient than a local travel agent.

● If you purchase your ticket from an airline Internet site you may not have complete flight information. Though Internet reservation systems have improved, their computer linkups are not as good as those used by travel agents connected directly to the airline computer reservation systems. Many times a travel agent can find a better fare. Until the Internet systems are brought into line with the travel agent systems such as Sabre, Worldspan and

Apollo, careful bargain-hunting Web surfers should check out Internet listed fares against what a good travel agent can discover.

● If you purchase your ticket through a travel agent you have more leeway for payment, since agencies normally make their payments to the airlines once a week. If you work frequently with a travel agent they will let you know their payment day—normally Tuesday at noon. They may sometimes cancel a ticket if you change your mind within a day or so. They can also place last-minute reservations before special fares expire and then bill you for the ticket, giving you about a week before you actually have to pay.

● If there is a problem, your travel agent is probably a member of the American Society of Travel Agents (ASTA) which has an excellent consumer protection program (see page 172).

What is a consolidator?

A consolidator is a discount airline ticket seller. Most of these operations are closely aligned with the major airlines. When normal airline deep-discounts still leave significant numbers of empty seats available on a given flight, the airlines release seats to consolidators who can sell these discounted tickets through travel agents, or in some cases directly to the public. You might call them the "factory outlets" of airlines. As with many discount stores, the names of the airlines are not advertised. You will be told of your airline choices before you purchase any tickets, and they will be clearly marked on your ticket.

Consolidators are not limited to no-name airlines. The world's largest airlines all sell tickets through consolidators. Though there are horror stories about consolidators, if you stick to the rule of using a credit card and working through a travel agent, there is nothing to fear, only bargains to be enjoyed.

▲ **NOTE**: Currently, most nonrefundable tickets purchased from airlines can be reapplied to another flight upon payment of a small fee if your plans change; consolidators may not allow that flexibility.

Consolidator fares normally are competitive with advance-purchase airfares; *however:* you do not have to purchase your ticket until the day of the flight if seats are still available. Your benefit is flexibility of purchase time, combined with advance-purchase pricing.

BE CAREFUL: Consolidator tickets may be more expensive than deep-discount promotions. Make sure to do your homework.

✔ **Consolidators have several drawbacks:**

● Depending on the type of ticket you purchase, you may not be eligible for frequent-flyer mileage credits or frequent-flyer upgrades.

● Your choice of airline and selection of available flight times are also limited. Also, with many consolidator tickets, seat assignments may only be given at flight time at the airport, and some of these tickets also preclude special meals (See page 35).

● Your ticket theoretically is only valid on the airline originally indicated on the ticket. If there is a flight cancellation or delay, you will either have to take a later flight on that airline, which may mean staying overnight, or purchase a full-fare ticket, eliminating any discount benefit. (Reportedly, some airlines have been known to make unofficial arrangements for stranded consolidator ticket holders, but don't bet on it.)

● Consolidator tickets cannot be refunded through the airlines—they must be refunded through the consolidator. In some cases they are nonrefundable. Buy consolidator tickets only with credit cards. If the consolidator goes bankrupt or fails to send you your ticket, you can cancel the charge.

● First- and business-class consolidator tickets are hard to find. Be careful when buying discount premium class fares to insure you are actually dealing with a consolidator rather than a frequent flyer coupon broker which involves significant risks.

● For more information on consolidators, ask your travel agent. They normally work with several consolidators for international and domestic travel. The *Consumer Reports Travel Letter* often reports on international and domestic airline consolidators and has back issues available.

Payments & Refunds on Airline Tickets

- If you plan to pay in person and with your own bank check, take along at least two forms of identification such as a driver's license, major credit card, and employee ID card. Airlines, travel agencies and other ticket sellers will want to confirm your identity, particularly when you purchase tickets far from your home town.

- If you pay for your ticket with cash or personal check, the ticket refund will generally have to be processed through the airline accounting department and mailed to you. The airlines have 20 business days—a calendar month—to process your refund.

- When you pay by credit card, your account is billed, whether you use your tickets or not. You won't receive credit unless the unused tickets are returned to the airline or travel agency, and you can't get a cash refund for a credit card charge. The credit card refund, however, is immediate.

- If you buy your ticket with a credit card and then change your flight, the ticket agent may want to credit the amount of the old ticket and issue another with a second charge to your account. You can insist that the value of your old tickets be applied to the new ones, with the difference in price charged or credited to your account. While this creates a little extra work for the airlines, it prevents double-billing on your card.

- When exchanging a nonrefundable airline ticket for another ticket, try to always exchange your ticket for another of equal or greater value. Some airlines are willing to exchange your nonrefundable ticket for another flight but they will not credit you with any differences in the cost of the ticket if the flight you plan to take does not cost as much as the original ticket.

● **NOTE:** You will almost always have to pay a $50 service fee to change or refund a ticket except in extreme cases.

● If you pay by credit card and have trouble getting a refund for a refundable ticket, report this *in writing* to your credit card company. If you write them within 60 days after they mailed your statement showing the charge for the ticket, they should credit your account.

● If the airline goes bankrupt, you can get a refund on your credit card. If you paid by cash or by check, there may be a very long and unfruitful wait.

● Most airline tickets are good for one year—after that time it may be difficult or impossible to get a refund.

Prepaying airline tickets

The short advice is don't prepay airline tickets for pickup at the airport. There is plenty that can go wrong and the airlines impose ridiculous fees. Prepaid ticket surcharges in early 1998 were already ranging from $75 on Delta and United to $40 on most other major airlines. You are better off having the ticket sent overnight to your home or business if your timetable makes it possible.

Changing tickets and refunding tickets for lower fares

We have all purchased an airline ticket only to find that the price dropped dramatically the next week or even the next day.

In these cases ticket holders may exchange their higher-priced ticket for the lower airfare. However, all the original restrictions of the original ticket must still apply, seats at the restricted fare must be available and you will be forced to pay a change fee of around $50–150 (normally $75 for U.S. domestic tickets).

For example: you just purchased a 14-day advanced fare ticket from Boston to Denver and opened the morning paper only to find a ticket for about $100 less. You can change the ticket if there are still 14 days before your flight and if there are still seats allocated for that fare. Call the airline or your travel agent and make another reservation at the new lower fare.

Here, a travel agent comes in very handy, since they can immediately change the ticket for the lower fare less any change fee. If you purchased your ticket from the airline, you will have to go to an airport or an airline ticket office to make the change. Or you could take your original ticket to a travel agent; the agent can cancel the ticket and issue you a new ticket providing a saving of $100 less the change fee.

NOTE: Travelers changing tickets can avoid these fees in some cases if they accept an airline voucher (airline script good for future flights or additional purchases from that airline). Naturally, a cash refund gives travelers more flexibility, but the airline vouchers mean you can get refunds for lower fares up to the last minute without taking more money out of your pocket.

Airline Ticket Contract Terms

A written contract between you and an airline is created every time you purchase a ticket. It is important to realize, however, that each airline has specific rules that make up what is called your Contract of Carriage. Your Contract of Carriage is not necessarily your ticket. The difference is explained below. These rules may differ between carriers. They include provisions such as check-in deadlines, limits on liability for lost baggage, responsibility for delayed flights, and many other considerations.

Originally, we planned to include a complete copy of a Contract of Carriage for one of the major airlines and one from a discount airline in an appendix of this book; however, each contract ran over 25 pages in this format. These contracts of carriage must be shown to passengers by ticketing personnel if requested. For some airlines, that is the only way to view these documents.

Some airlines publish their Contract of Carriage on the Internet. Three of these are United Airlines, Southwest Airlines and Reno Air.

United Airlines does not make their Contract of Carriage easy to find. It can not be found in their normal Internet site, but is online at http://www.sirius.com/~eps/UA/UA/dgr-1/Welcome.html. The Southwest and Reno Contracts of Carriage are easily discovered in their normal Web sites. The Southwest page is http://www.iflyswa.com/info/contract.html. The Reno Air page is http://www.renoair.com/GeneralInfo/Contract.html.

Airlines are required to show passengers these complete terms in writing if they ask. **NOTE:** Do not assume the Contract Terms for United Airlines are the same as those for United Express. Contract Terms for "Express" divisions of airlines, such as United Express (in effect independent regional airlines), are significantly different from the parent airline.

Domestic travel

For domestic travel, some airlines provide all contract terms on or with your ticket at the time you buy it. Many small commuter carriers use this system. Other airlines may elect to "incorporate terms by reference" into their contracts of carriage for domestic transportation. You are not given all the airline's rules with your ticket—most of them are contained in a separate document that you can inspect on request.

If an airline elects to incorporate by reference it must provide conspicuous written notice with each ticket that:

1) it incorporates terms by reference, and

2) these terms may include liability limitations, claim-filing deadlines, check-in deadlines, and certain other key terms; the airline must also:

● Insure that passengers can receive an explanation of key terms identified on the ticket from any location where the carrier's tickets are sold, including travel agencies;

● Make available for inspection the full text of its Contract of Carriage at each of its own airport and city ticket offices; and

● Mail a free copy of the full Contract of Carriage upon *written* request.

There are additional notice requirements for contract terms that affect your airfare. Airlines must provide a

conspicuous written notice on or with the ticket concerning any "incorporated" contract terms that:

● Restrict refunds;

● Impose monetary penalties; or

● Permit the airline to raise the price after you've
bought the ticket.

If a U.S. airline incorporates contract terms by reference
and fails to provide the required notice about a particular rule, the passenger will not be bound by that
rule.

Ticketless travel

In these days of electronic ticketing, passengers taking advantage of the electronic ticket will not receive
a Contact of Carriage until they arrive at the airport to
pick up their boarding passes. In some cases the electronic ticketing process does not provide any contract.
Sometimes the mailed itinerary will include a Contract
of Carriage. Check carefully. While most consumers
have the right to, and normally insist on reading a contract before signing it, the airlines expect you to sign
away all rights without even being allowed a chance
to read the Contract of Carriage.

International travel

The detailed requirements for disclosing domestic contract terms do not apply to international travel. Airlines file Tariff Rules with the government for international service. Passengers are generally bound by these
rules whether or not they receive actual notice of them.

Every international airline must keep a copy of its tariff rules at its airport and city ticket offices. You have a
right to examine these rules. The airline agents must

answer your questions about information in the tariff, and they must help you locate specific tariff rules, if necessary.

The most important point to remember, whether your travel is domestic or international, is that you should not be afraid to ask questions about an airline's rules. You have a right to know the terms of your Contract of Carriage. It is in your best interest, as well as the airline's, for you to ask in advance about any matters of uncertainty.

Charter rights

Originally, this section dealt with what were obviously charter flights. However, in this day and age, several low-fare carriers are actually Public Charters in disguise. Make sure you know whether you are flying on a "scheduled carrier" or a "charter flight." The federal regulation differences are mind-boggling. On charter flights, passengers give up virtually all their rights to immediate redress and place themselves in a poor position for any compensation should anything go wrong with a flight. Be careful. Know the charter operators and know their records. These are flights that can be a bargain, but if anything goes wrong, all savings can quickly evaporate.

Charter flights are governed by rules far different from those that regulate scheduled airline carriers. For every dollar you save, there may be another price to pay. Often charter prices are only a few dollars less than those of scheduled airlines. This next section was published by the DOT as part of its Plane Talk series to tell consumers what "Charter" really entails. It does not take a rocket scientist to see that these rules favor the charter operators and not the passengers.

Over the past few years, charter flights have been relaxed to make lower cost air transportation available to more people. Public Charters can be purchased from a tour operator, a travel agent, or sometimes directly from the airline.

If your flight has been arranged by a club or other organization for its members it may be what is called an affinity charter flight. These charters generally do not carry the consumer protection provisions of Public Charters. Be sure you know what kind of charter flight you are purchasing.

A Public Charter may include only the flight, or it may be sold as a complete package, including hotels, guided tours, and ground transportation. Either way, your rights are spelled out in a contract you have with the tour operator. The operator or your travel agent should give you a contract to sign at the time you purchase your trip. Read it before you pay any money.

The Department of Transportation requires tour operators to disclose certain information in your contract about the restrictions that they impose and also rights that you have under DOT rules:

❑ **You usually pay penalties if you cancel.** The closer to departure you cancel, the bigger the penalty. On some charters, if a substitute can go in your place you only lose a $25 fee.

❑ **You can buy trip cancellation insurance.** These policies usually provide a refund in case you must cancel owing to illness or death in the family. Your travel agent or tour operator can tell you how to buy the insurance and what health conditions it does or doesn't cover. Charter cancellation insurance often won't pay you if you must cancel because of a preexisting condition.

❑ **A Public Charter can be cancelled for any reason up until 10 days before departure.** The flight might be canceled if it doesn't sell well or for another reason. This is a risk you take in return for a low fare. (During the last 10 days before departure, a Public Charter can be canceled only if it is physically impossible to operate it.)

❐ **All charter flights and ground arrangements are subject to changes.** Signing a contract does not guarantee that prices won't go up or that itineraries won't change. But, if there is a *major change* in your flight or tour, *you have the right to cancel and get a penalty-free refund.*

Major changes include:

❐ A change in departure or return city (not including a simple change in the order in which cities are visited).

❐ A change in departure or return date, unless the date change results from a flight delay. (However, a flight delay of more than <u>48 hours</u> is a major change.)

❐ A substitution of a hotel that was not named as an alternative hotel in your contract.

❐ An increase in price, if the total of all increases billed to you is more than 10 percent of what you originally paid. (No increases are allowed during the last 10 days before departure.)

If your tour operator notifies you of a major change before departure, you get a full refund if you decide to cancel. If you choose not to cancel, the operator is not required to make partial refunds. However, if you don't find out about a change until after your trip has begun, you can reject the changed flight or hotel, make and pay for your own alternative plans, and insist on a refund for the changed component when you get home.

❏ **No "open returns" are allowed on round-trip public charters.** Be sure you have a specific return date, city and flight, so you won't be stranded.

❏ **The tour operator has to take specific steps to protect your money.** They must have a surety agreement, such as a bond, and must usually have an escrow account at a bank that holds your money until your flight takes place. If your money is going into a charter escrow account, the bank will be named in your contract, and the check that is sent to the charter operator should be made payable to that bank. (If you are using a travel agent, it's OK for you to make your check out to that agent; he will make his check payable to the escrow account.) Identify the departure date and destination on the check. If a tour operator goes out of business you should contact the surety company or bank identified in your contract for a refund.

❏ **You alone are responsible for knowing if you need a visa and passport for your trip.** You can be certain of the visa and passport rules of the countries you plan to visit by calling or writing their embassies in Washington, D.C., or their consulates in some major U.S. cities.

❏ **If your luggage gets lost during your tour, there may be a dispute over who is liable.** The charter airlines process claims for bags that were lost or damaged while in their possession. If it is not clear where the problem occurred (e.g. between the airport and a hotel), the operator and the airline may both decline liability. To cover yourself, find out if your renter's or homeowner's insurance policy covers losses that happen when you're away from home. You might also ask your travel agent if there's a one-shot baggage insurance policy available to cover baggage problems while you are on your charter trip.

❐ **Your charter may be delayed.** Last minute schedule changes and departure delays of several hours are not uncommon. A flight can be delayed up to 48 hours before the charter operator must offer you the option to cancel with a full refund.

❐ **Charters and scheduled flights operate independently of each other.** If there's a delay on the scheduled flight connecting you to the city where your charter departs, causing you to miss your charter, you lose your flight and money. Charter reservations are only good for one flight. If you miss it for any reason, you're probably out of luck. Check with the tour operator to see if he has another charter flying to your destination.

If your charter is late returning and causes you to miss a scheduled connecting flight back to your home, you have to pay your own expenses while you wait for the next connection. If you have a discount fare on a scheduled connecting flight you could lose it if the returning charter is delayed. Then you, not the airline or tour operator, have to pay more for a regular non-discount fare.

Your baggage can't be checked through from a scheduled flight to a charter, and vice-versa. You have to claim your baggage and recheck it yourself. When planning a charter, allow plenty of time to check in at the airport from which your charter leaves, or from which you have a connecting flight. On international trips, remember that you may encounter delays in customs.

❐ **You might find the seating on your charter plane more crowded than you're used to.** The low charter rate depends in part on spreading costs over a large number of people with virtually all of the seats being filled.

❐ **If a charter flight hasn't sold out shortly before departure, the operator can sell seats at bargain basement prices to latecomers.** Some who have paid the regular price well in advance may object, but should realize that the operator's alternative may be to cancel the flight altogether.

❐ **Charter rates are relatively low, but may not be the cheapest fare.** Ask your travel agent to compare fares on scheduled and charter flights for you.

Charters offer nonstop flights for an affordable price. They can be a wise travel investment if you can be flexible in your travel plans. Just be sure you know the conditions for the trip you're buying before you pay for it. Questions? Call DOT at 202-366-2220.

✔ **AUTHOR'S NOTE:** My vote is to pay the small amount of extra money needed to take a scheduled flight.

Reservations and Tickets

Once you decide where you want to go, and about when, you can begin the reservation and ticketing process. You can make all your arrangements through a travel agent, other ticket marketer, by telephone directly with the airline, online using a Web reservation system or at the airline's ticket office. There are a few potential pitfalls, however, and these pointers should help you avoid them.

- If your travel falls into a busy period, call for reservations early. Flights for holidays may sell out weeks—sometimes months—ahead of time.

- When you make a reservation, be sure the airline records the information accurately. Before you hang up or leave the ticket office, review all of the essential information with the agent—the spelling of your name, the flight numbers and travel dates, and the cities you are traveling between. If there is more than one airport at either city, be sure to check which one you'll be using. It's also important to give the airline your home and work telephone numbers so that they can let you know about any changes in the schedule.

- Whenever you call an airline to make reservations or purchase a ticket, get the reservation locator number, confirmation number, or PNR code. This number makes it much easier to settle any future questions that may arise about your reservation. If you have your ticket, this number can be found in the box above the first flight.

● Your ticket will show the flight numbers, departure times and dates, and status of your reservations for each leg of your itinerary. The "status" box is important. "OK" means you're confirmed, "HK" can mean the same thing (Hold Confirm). Anything else means you're only wait-listed or that the reservation is not yet certain.

● When an agent says you must buy your tickets by a specific time or date, this is a deadline. If you don't purchase your ticket before the deadline, the airline may cancel your reservations without further notification.

● If your reservations are booked far enough ahead of time, the airline may offer to mail your tickets. Otherwise, check the telephone directory for the nearest ticket office or travel agency and buy your tickets there or head to a travel agency.

● Try to have your tickets in hand before you go to the airport or travel "ticketless." This is smart traveling. It helps avoid some of the tension you may otherwise feel if you have to wait in a slow-moving ticket line and worry about missing your flight.

Ticketless travel

The airlines have introduced "ticketless travel." The effort is to reduce the amount of paper generated by the ticketing process and to take advantage of computer technology.

Once a ticketless travelers have purchased an airline ticket, they are sent a confirmation letter in the mail. This confirmation provides written evidence that they have indeed purchased a ticket. However, travelers do not need this paper to pick up boarding passes at the airport. As long as travelers have their confirmation number or can remember their flight number and name, they can check their baggage at the curbside baggage check and then walk directly to the departure gate.

In some cases passengers traveling "ticketless" will be required, for security purposes, to stop at the ticket counter to pick up a boarding pass before heading to the departure gate.

When traveling during crowded holiday periods, I recommend having the airlines send full tickets and boarding passes. Even with the magic of computers and the apparent ease of traveling "ticketless," the airlines' policy of overbooking can make it far better to have clear evidence in the form of an advanced boarding pass that a specific seat on a specific flight has been assigned for your travel.

One excellent point of ticketless travel is that it is impossible to lose your ticket, so problems with lost tickets disappear.

Code sharing

International and domestic airlines over the recent years have developed marketing alliances that allow them to offer "seamless travel" between Europe, Asia, the United States and Africa on separate airlines. Code sharing, which started with the KLM/Northwest landmark partnership, opened the door allowing one airline to sell seats, that they claim as their own, on another airline's aircraft as well as coordinate flights and service to insure the best-possible connections.

For instance, if you purchase a ticket for a KLM flight from Boston to Zürich you will check in at a joint KLM/Northwest counter. Then, though your ticket clearly states the flight is on KLM, you will board a Northwest jet for the flight from Boston to Amsterdam. The connecting flight will be on a KLM jet from Amsterdam to Zürich.

In the beginning, this airline coordination was touted as a way to improve passenger service. Code sharing allowed coordinated schedules on international flights theoretically to make the travel experience more hassle-free. The concept is now being expanded to include coordination of domestic airline schedules between separate airlines. In the code-share world, coordinating schedules and marketing is the easy part. Developing similar standards of service to be shared between foreign and domestic airlines has proven much more difficult. Reality has proven that service improvements have been minimal, but airline bottom line improvements have been significant.

Code sharing works when the airlines are more or less well matched such as Northwest and KLM where the crews and passengers all speak good English. Problems and confusion arise when passengers expecting to fly on a Continental flight end up flying on Alitalia; Swissair passengers find themselves on Delta or Austrian Airlines; and German-speakers have to deal with United Airlines flight attendants when they were expecting to fly on a Lufthansa plane. This mixing of airlines is only going to get worse before someone steps in to calm the madness.

Theoretically, in the United States, reservation agents are required to inform passengers of flights that are sold under the name of one airline and flown on aircraft owned by another, but in most cases the passenger must know enough to ask. Otherwise, the reservation agent may forget.

NEGOTIATING THROUGH THE AIRFARE MAZE

The rule these days is to compare. Never accept the first fare quoted. Many times, another flight on another airline within an hour of the time you want to fly will provide a less expensive deal. If you have time before the final advanced-purchase date and are faced with what you feel is a high "lowest rate," you might wait a couple of days and try to make the reservation again when the "lowest available fare" may have been lowered or more seats allocated for that fare.

When purchasing an airline ticket for my mother recently for a flight from the Southeast to Boston, I was quoted a price of around $280 for a round-trip 21-day advanced purchase senior-citizen ticket. I told the reservation agent thank you, but decided to wait and try making the reservation again the following week. When I called a week later, the same flights were still available and the price had dropped to $181.

The more flexibility travelers have and the earlier they begin to make reservations are major factors in negotiating the airfare maze. Remember, when a reservation agent informs you that all low-priced tickets have been sold, they are telling you what the situation is at that moment. Within hours, minutes, even seconds there may be seats opening up at the low price you wanted to purchase. Another traveler may have canceled a reservation or failed to pay for their reservation, the airline may have decided to make more discounted seats available or the size of the airplane may have changed. These are only a few of the factors that affect airline ticket prices and availability.

Most airlines have more than a dozen different types of fares for domestic flights and as many as 75 in various international markets. But there are some basic fare groups that serve as a starting point for breaking them down.

The three classes offer the principal breakdown of fares and are operated as separately as possible from each other.

✈ **First Class** is the top-of-the-line service with wide seats (some that fully recline), sometimes beds, and meals far too extensive and rich for any normal traveler to consume, served on fine china with silverware, all accompanied by flasks of vintage wine and champagne as well as port, cognac and liqueurs.

✈ **Business Class** is normally a significant step below First Class. Here seats are not as large nor do they recline as far, you won't find beds, and the wines and spirits are far more pedestrian. (Some airlines are now eliminating First Class and replacing it with a souped-up Business Class.)

✈ **Coach Class** is the back of the plane. Here seats are narrow with only minimal reclining possibilities. Meals on most airlines are served on plastic and consumed with similar utensils. On U.S. carriers flying domestically, you usually pay for any beverage other than basic juices, carbonated sodas and water. Some U.S. airlines do provide free alcoholic drinks on international flights. On foreign airlines, a bottle of wine or beer is often included in the Coach Class price when flying within Europe and free beverage service is the norm when flying intercontinental.

Within each of these classes there are many fare variations. At this point the important fact to remember is that the fares you would pay—if you merely walked up to the counter and purchased a ticket for a flight on that same day—are nothing short of mind-boggling high. **So you have to plan ahead.**

With planning, travelers can take advantage of tickets such as:

- ✈ 21- to 14-day advance purchase
- ✈ 7-day advance purchase
- ✈ round-trip Saturday-night stayover
- ✈ deep-discount tickets (often called supersavers)
- ✈ and more . . .

For the information you need to negotiate this pricing maze, you can contact a travel agent, an airline serving the places you want to visit, or a consolidator (see page 19). With a little research in local papers, by telephone or on computer services, you can find all airlines flying to your destination. Then you can call each airline to ask about their fares and any special deals they may offer. You can also watch the newspapers where airlines advertise many of their most heavily discounted plans. Finally, be alert to new companies serving the market. They may offer lower fares than older established airlines.

Here are some tips and questions to ask to help you decide between airfares:

● Be flexible in your travel plans if you want the lowest fare. Often there are complicated conditions you must meet to qualify for a discount. The most usual requirement is that you purchase your ticket at least 21 or 14 days in advance (sometimes seven days in advance, sometimes less) and stay over a Saturday night.

- Ask the reservation agent for the lowest fare on the route you want to book. Phrase it like this, "What is the absolutely lowest fare on this route assuming I had plenty of time and ultimate flexibility, what are the restrictions for that fare?" Then ask, "What is the next best fare and its restrictions." If you must travel on a certain day, ask for "the lowest fare available for travel on that day, regardless of time of departure." Once you get those answers, you can make decisions. Either shift your flights to dates and times that allow for the lowest fares, or pay more for convenience.

- Plan as far ahead as you can. Some airlines set aside only a few seats on each flight at the low rates, so that the real bargains often sell out very quickly. (But you can keep trying—the airline may change, and do change, the number of deep-discount seats several times during any promotion.)

- Some airlines may have discounts that others don't offer. In a large metropolitan area, the fare could depend on which airport you use.

- Does the airfare include types of service that airlines have traditionally provided, such as meals or free baggage handling? (Many of the low-fare scheduled airlines only serve snacks and soda, and they normally do not participate in what is called interlining of baggage—the transfer of bags between airlines.)

- If you are stranded, will the ticket be good on another airline at no extra charge? Will the first airline pay for meals or hotel rooms?

- Find out what will happen if you decide to switch flights. Will you lose the benefit of your discount fare? Are there any cancellation fees? Is there a cutoff date for making and changing reservations without paying more money?

● Some airlines will not increase the fare after the ticket is issued and paid for. (*However*, merely holding a reservation without a ticket does not guarantee the fare.) Before you buy your ticket, ask if the airline can increase the fare later.

● Remember, when you purchase a nonrefundable ticket, the ticket is what the name implies—nonrefundable, even only two hours later (unless you use a travel agent—see *Why a travel agent can help* section). Most airlines, however, will allow you to apply the cost of the ticket to another ticket on their airline (after deducting around a $50–150 handling fee).

● Differences in airfare can be substantial. Careful comparison shopping between airlines does take time, but it can lead to real savings.

Rules that apply to charter flights are covered in the *Charter Rights* section

Reconfirming flights

✔ It's a good idea to reconfirm your reservations before each flight on your trip; flight schedules sometimes change. On international trips, most airlines require that you reconfirm your onward or return reservations at least 72 hours before each flight. If you don't, your reservations may be canceled. We recommend that every international traveler always reconfirm, since some airlines are much more rigid on this requirement than others.

Don't be a "no-show." If you are holding confirmed reservations you don't plan to use, notify the airline as soon as you're definite about not taking that flight.

Back-to-back fares and hidden city fares

For most vacation travelers, these tactics rarely result in a savings over the normal advanced purchase airline ticket. But for business travelers, there can often be a significant savings. These strategies are against the airlines' rules, but enforcement of them is difficult and in many cases, up until press time, the airline reservation agents often sold back-to-back airline tickets themselves.

Hidden city fares come into play when a traveler wants to fly from Boston to Denver for instance. Many times the Boston–Denver airfare is more expensive than purchasing a Boston to Los Angeles ticket with a stop or change of planes in Denver. During the stop, the passenger simply heads into Denver, abandoning the Denver to Los Angeles portion of the airfare. This only works with carry-on luggage since airline personnel will not check bags only for a portion of any flight.

Back-to-back fares or nesting is a way around what is called the Saturday-night rule. Deep-discounted tickets provide significant savings, but they require that the airline passenger stay over a Saturday night. This was to discourage high-fare business travelers from buying low-fare leisure-travel tickets: the Saturday-night rule meant the businessmen either had to stay away from their families over the weekends or fork over higher fares.

Provided you are traveling to the same destination at least twice within the same fare period, nesting will allow you to purchase one round-trip ticket from your home and a second round-trip ticket from your destination and nest them to circumvent the Saturday-night rule.

You need at least two round-trip tickets to nest.

Example:

1. Fly Boston to Dallas Monday morning with your first round-trip ticket.

2. Return to Boston Friday with the second round-trip ticket.

3. The following Monday, leave again for Dallas using the return portion of your second round-trip ticket.

4. Return to Boston on Friday with the return portion of your first ticket.

Airlines have begun to scream about this tactic and some have sent fines and debit memos to travel agents who write these types of tickets, but as mentioned above, the airline's own reservation agents will often book back-to-back tickets.

The airline/travel agent contract is far different from the airline/passenger relationship. The former is a business contract with explicit rules and agreements. The latter is a contract for carriage where most of the rules are difficult to obtain and virtually never presented prior to purchase. Should the airlines begin to take out advertising notifying passengers of the "contract" to which they agree when they purchase an airline ticket, this relationship may change.

After consulting with travel agents and lawyers, the best way to insure that there is no violation of rules is to book the two round-trip tickets with different airlines. For an airline to require that you use both halves of a round trip airline ticket is similar to having a soft drink company require that anyone who purchases a 20 oz. bottle of cola must drink the whole bottle. Once you purchase an airline ticket, you own it. If you never fly anywhere and keep it in your drawer, that is not against the law.

Purchase two round-trip airline tickets from two different airlines, then use only half of each ticket. That is not against the law. Travelers are only buying what the airlines offer for sale to the public.

Fortunately, as discount airlines begin to expand, these Saturday night stayover rules and exorbitant full fares may become less important and travelers will not have to manipulate the system to get a fair deal.

✔ Examine or have your travel agent carefully examine discount supersaver airfares if you are planning a trip seven to 21 days in advance, but can't stay over a Saturday night. You will often find that it is less expensive to purchase two separate round-trip supersaver tickets, discarding the *return* portions of each, rather than buy a standard coach round trip.

Alternate cities

This money-saving technique seems obvious, however many travelers overlook its benefits. To take advantage of lower fares, simply check out airfares to and from nearby airports. For instance Boston to Chicago is a very expensive business fare ticket; however if a traveler departed from Providence, RI, only an hour's drive from Boston, the walk-up fare to Chicago is less than any advanced purchase fare available from Boston.

Alternate city techniques work well in cities such as Boston, New York, Washington D.C., Chicago, San Francisco or Los Angeles where there are several airports within an hour of downtown. Fares for flights in and out of La Guardia are often higher than flights serving J.F.K. or Newark. Dulles and B.W.I. often provide discounts when compared with Washington National.

Take advantage of return date flexibility and standby rules

The outbound segment of a round-trip advance-purchase ticket is cast in stone as far as the date of travel, but the return date has lots of flexibility. Most airlines will allow travelers to change the return date for a fee of $50 or so. Most passengers can also fly standby on a different date for no additional charge as long as the Saturday-night-stay requirement has been met. So, make your plans today to lock in a lower fare rather than wait for exact travel dates. Changing the return dates is not a big deal and can save bundles over paying a walk-up fare.

Using coupons

One of the most widely spread discount programs that virtually every airline uses is couponing. These coupons come from shopping malls with a purchase of $25 worth of merchandise, they come in the mail together with takeout Chinese restaurant menus, they show up in credit card bills and with frequent flyer materials. Sometimes, the airline discount coupon that comes with a purchase of a low-cost item makes buying the product a no-brainer. Coupons can be like found money. The discounts are normally excellent, providing transportation for far less than advance-purchase tickets.

Coupons have an additional benefit that most flyers overlook—they are transferable. Most airlines will honor the coupons of competitors. So, if you may have a coupon on airline A but prefer to fly on airline B, you can often use one airline's coupon on a competing airline. Not all coupons are transferable, but the majority of them are. Frequent flyer coupons are an important exception to this rule.

The most important information on a coupon is the fine print. Here, you will find the restrictions and rules for obtaining your discount. These are important—no matter with which airline you attempt to cash in the coupon, these restrictions will stay in effect. You may have to mail in a request for the actual coupon, pay a handling fee, deal with blackout dates, and travel with another person or from specific airports.

Senior fares

Those over the age of 62 have one of the best bargains in the airline industry with their senior coupons. Though the coupon airfares are not always lower than supersaver fares for short hauls, they are convenient and easy to use. Also, many airlines add a 10 percent senior discount to even the deepest discount ticket; others have a separate senior citizen fare structure. For long-haul tickets there are few better deals.

Currently some of the major airlines are developing senior "clubs" with ticketing based on travel between "zones." Some of these programs allow first class travel, others don't. Some of these programs permit international travel, some don't. Some of these "club" tickets allow companions of any age to travel on identical itineraries, others don't. Some have minimum stay requirements or Saturday night stayover provisions, others don't. As currently structured these programs require reservations 14 days in advance and all seats are capacity controlled.

☞ Some senior coupon highlights:

● Some airlines allow companions (any age) of seniors to fly with a senior coupon. At press time, Air Canada and TWA had this liberal policy. USAirways limits companions to ages 2 to 11.

- In Canada you only have to be aged 60 to qualify for senior coupons.

- Most senior coupons give frequent-flyer credit, except TWA.

- If you need a wheelchair or agent assistance, make your request at the same time as your reservation. Check again when you arrive at the airport and have airline personnel call ahead to your destination or connection.

Bereavement fares (Domestic U.S.)

These fares are for people who must travel to a funeral or visit a sick relative. There are no firm and fast rules for these fares in the industry.

These fares are normally not as inexpensive as super-saver fares or advance-purchase coach fares, but they are much less expensive than the normal last-minute purchase-at-the-counter business traveler fares. When a low-fare airline offers flights to your emergency destination, their unrestricted fares are often less expensive than major airline bereavement or compassionate fares.

Since the formula for bereavement fares varies so much from airline to airline, you should check the rates of all airlines that offer service to your destination and find out what documentation, if any, is required to secure the bereavement fare.

When you call be sure to be able to document your bereavement or emergency. Ask specific questions about the fares. However, in this case, the reservationist will probably ask you the questions to see if you qualify for the bereavement or compassionate fares. Each airline has its own rules. Some only allow for these fares in case of death (and require a death certificate or obituary notice for reimbursement), others provide discounts for visiting family members during medical emergencies. Some airlines require that family members be physically in a hospital, others allow a simple doctor's note indicating that you should return to help with the medical emergency.

Some airlines require that you pay full fare, but state that you will receive a partial rebate after the trip. Find out if the rebate is in cash or merely in the form of vouchers for future travel.

Bereavement fares (International)

Many U.S. airlines do not have bereavement fare policies for passengers traveling internationally. If a traveler must return to the United States or their home country while traveling abroad make sure to check with the airline. This is an area where you are dependent on an understanding customer service representative, supervisor or station chief.

The worst case is that you will be required to pay the full fare for your return flight. The best case is that the airline will allow you to use your ticket to return home standby if there is space available.

If you must initiate international travel at the last minute because of illness in your immediate family. Follow the same procedures as you would domestically. Since the international fare structure is much more restricted by international fare agreements, airlines do not have as much room to maneuver as in the United States. Many airlines, however, will waive the advanced purchase restrictions and allow bereaved passengers or those who must rush bedside a signifi-cant discount from the full international airfare.

Once again, be ready with a funeral home phone num-ber, a doctor's phone number, or the phone number of the hospital where your sick relative is staying.

International air passes and visitor tickets

Another deal that travelers can use when touring Eu-rope or the South Pacific are the visitor airfares and air passes. These virtually all consist of a set of flight coupons that are valid for a one-way flight. They are sold in blocks of coupons and may or may not turn out to be a bargain depending on travel plans. Some of these coupon programs allow one coupon for con-necting flights, others require two coupons if there is a connection. The bottom line—ask questions and understand how these "passes" work before purchas-ing them.

These passes and visitor tickets have specific limita-tions: some must be purchased before any trans-At-lantic flight and virtually all are linked with the pur-chase of a trans-Atlantic airline ticket. Their rates vary on time of the year and travel zones in some cases.

In Europe there are country passes for France, Finland, Norway and Spain. The *Le France Pass* on Air Inter al-lows seven days of unlimited air travel in France within one month for under $340 at press time. They also offer a student/youth pass for an even greater saving.

There also are regional passes, which are really cou-pon programs, from SAS for Scandinavia, and Scandinavia and the Baltics; and from Alitalia and Air Sicilia for Italy and some Middle East destinations.

- Europe-wide passes limited to the respective airline's route network are available from various airline groups.

- SAS Visit Europe is SAS's Europe-wide coupon program. It also includes flights to Tel Aviv.

- The Visit Europe pass provides travel on Austrian Airlines, Sabena, Swissair, Crossair and Tyrolean Airlines.

- Europe Airpass offers flights on the British Airways route with three smaller partners.

- Discover Europe Airpass radiates from Britain on British Midland airline.

- EuroPass is the coupon program of Iberia linked with transatlantic tickets from abroad to Spain.

- Passport to Europe is a partnership between KLM and Northwest with travel to more than 90 cities. Coupons are valid on travel with Air UK, Transavia, Tyrolean, Maersk Áir and Eurowings as well as with KLM and Northwest. It must be purchased in the U.S. prior to travel and offers child and infant discounts.

- Discover Europe Pass is used on flights of Lufthansa, Finnair and several smaller airlines.

- Euro Flyer Pass is a coupon program linking Air France, Air Inter and Czech airlines covering about 100 destinations.

- Hungarian Pass to Europe links Malev and Alitalia flights in Europe hubbing in Budapest.

- Finnair had a Holiday Ticket valid for 30 days to your choice of over 20 Finnish destinations.

- In the South Pacific various air passes and coupon programs provide a way to travel in the regions between the tropical islands, Australia and New Zealand (and in some cases Hawaii). Each program is different and must be purchased before arriving in the region.

● There are other programs that provide coupon travel within only Australia or New Zealand and between the two countries. Ansett offers the widest variety of the coupon programs.

● Some programs only link tropical islands and exclude travel to and from Australia and New Zealand.

● All these passes are normally valid for economy travel and offer child and infant discounts ranging from 67 percent to 10 percent of the adult airfare.

● If you are traveling to India, Thailand and Indonesia, passes are available as well.

● South America is covered by various passes offered by Avensa Airlines, Aeroperu, Avianca, LAN ChileAerolinas Argentina.

Infants, Children & Unaccompanied Minors

Infant fares

Children through age 2 do not require tickets for domestic travel in the U.S., however, they will not be given an assigned seat nor any baggage allowance unless you purchase a ticket for them. If the plane is full, any child 2 years or younger will be expected to sit on an accompanying adult's lap.

Several airlines are now offering discounted infant fares to allow the use of a child seat as well reservations and an increased baggage allowance. Discounts for the additional seats to be used by infants in an infant seat are normally 50 percent.

On international flights, children aged 2 and younger are required to pay 10 percent of the adult fare. They receive no benefits, seat or baggage allowance for that payment.

NOTE: While traveling internationally, solo parents traveling with children must carry a letter of consent from the absent parent. Carry these letters especially when traveling to Mexico, Canada, South America and Australia.

HAVE YOUR PAPERS AND YOUR CHILD'S PAPERS IN ORDER. OFFICIALS AT INTERNATIONAL BORDERS CAN BE VERY PICKY ABOUT THESE DOCUMENTS.

Infants and infant seats

Infant seats are now recommended, *not required*, by the Federal Aviation Administration, but in most cases, you'll have to pay full fare for the seat your child occupies to reserve and guarantee a place.

If the infant seat is not FAA-approved, some airlines will not allow you to bring it aboard—you may wish to ask the airline for a list of approved infant seats. However, with the exception of homemade car seats or baby feeder seats, almost every car seat manufactured today meets FAA standards. Call the FAA (see p. 137) for their booklet, *Child/Infant Safety Seats Recommended for Use in Aircraft*.

There are several options for avoiding the purchase of an extra ticket for an infant:

● Hold the child on your lap during the flight. If you do this, children under the age of 2 can fly free domestically and for 10 percent of full adult fare internationally. One "carry-on" child is allowed per adult.

● NOTE: The 10 percent you pay for an infant on an international flight does not pay for a guaranteed seat—you still are expected to hold the child on your lap should the flight be full.

● Some parents prefer a bulkhead seat with a bassinet. The bassinet can be used after takeoff for small infants, but you still must hold the infant on your lap for takeoff and landing. Make your request for a bassinet early. Some airlines are more helpful with bassinets than others. Ask other parents about their experiences.

● Many parents feel bulkhead seats are undesirable since there is no under-seat storage, the armrests don't fold up and down, and some don't have tables. Unless you are using a bassinet, another seat may be best.

- Bring your own infant seat with you on the plane and hope for an empty seat next to you. Most airlines will allow you to use the infant seat on a space-available basis. But the seat must be small enough to fit under your seat or in an overhead compartment should the seat next to yours not be empty.

- Purchase an infant ticket. At press time most major airlines had no infant fare; however, that may change in the near future—ask. (Southwest Airlines was the only carrier with an infant fare— about 60 percent of the adult fare—that will guarantee a seat.)

- Most major airlines *will reserve the seat next to you* if you are traveling with an infant. That seat will only be used if the flight is full.

- Bring your own infant food or ask the airline specifically whether baby-food meals are available. Call at least 24 hours in advance.

TWYCH—Travel With Your Children, based in New York, publishes an excellent detailed *Airline Guide* for children's travel with details on most major airlines, for both accompanied and unaccompanied children.

Subscribers to *Family Travel Times* get one free; nonsubscribers may purchase a copy of the latest edition for $10 plus $2 postage and handling by sending a check to: TWYCH, 40 Fifth Avenue, New York, NY 10011.

Child fares

Passengers who have reached their second birthday are expected to pay the applicable adult fare.

✔ As noted above, on some airlines senior citizens with senior coupons (meaning Grandma or Grandpa for the most part) with a child under the age of 11 can also use a senior coupon for the child's fare. Many of the 10 percent senior reductions are also available to companions traveling with seniors.

Internationally there is a bit more of a break on ticket prices, with children aged 2 to 11 paying 50 to 75 percent of the applicable fare.

In Europe there are Youth Fares available that offer semi-standby travel for youths aged 12 to 24. These seats normally are only confirmed within 72 hours of departure for both legs of a trip, so they offer plenty of flexibility.

In the U.S., Youth Fares are few and far between. TWA offers a coupon program and other airlines have specials offered at various times during the year.

Unaccompanied minors

Though the charges are the same for minors and adults, the rights to travel are not. On most airlines, unaccompanied children under the age of 5 are not permitted.

Unaccompanied minors 5 to 7 years of age may be accepted on a nonstop or through flight and must be accompanied by a responsible adult until the child is boarded. The child must be met by a responsible adult.

On most U.S. airlines, unaccompanied children 8 through 11 years of age may be accepted on nonstop, through or connecting flights. Reservations must be confirmed to the destination. Children making connections will be assisted by the airline (if your child is changing *airlines*, make sure airline personnel will "hand off" your child to the next carrier—most won't, so plan on a single airline flight). Again, the child must be accompanied by a responsible adult until boarding and met by a responsible adult with proper identification upon arriving.

Unaccompanied children 12 through 17 years of age may receive assistance making connecting flights upon request.

Most airlines charge an additional fee of $20–30 to escort a child onto another plane when making connections.

If you are sending a young child on an airline journey alone, check the airline policy.

✔ Tips for parents sending their children on a flight:

● Try to make the reservations on a nonstop or direct flight. In some cases this is required.

● Introduce your child to the gate agent and REMIND the agent that your child will need assistance changing planes when appropriate.

● Let the cabin crew know if this is the child's first flight—they will do their best to reassure the child.

● Do not book your child on the last flight of the evening. In the event of a delay or missed connection the child will have to spend the night alone in a strange city.

● Tuck in a pocket or in a pouch around the child's neck all identification information, with the child's name and destination, the flight numbers and schedule, your name, your address, your phone number, and whether any luggage was checked. (The Travel Card on the next page provides a good outline of information.)

● Give the child some spending money for movie headsets, phone calls, or food in case of a delay. Let them know what is free and what they have to pay for.

● Try to get a window seat.

● Give your child games and books to help keep him or her occupied during the flight.

● Order a child's meal 4 to 24 hours in advance, depending on the airline.

● Let children know who will be picking them up at the airport when they arrive.

● Tell the person picking up your child on the other end of the flight to bring proper identification. No airline will release a child without it. Children will only be released to adults listed on a travel card or the Unaccompanied Minor Forms, provided by the airline.

● Call ahead to let the folks meeting the flight know what time the plane actually took off.

TRAVEL CARD

SEAT #

Name of child:

Age:

Name of sender:

Address:

Telephone: Day

       Evening

Name of Receiver:

Address:

Telephone: Day

       Evening

Airline Information

Airline: Flight #

Destination   **Ticket #**

Departure Time   **Arrival Time**

List of connecting flights

Airline Flight #

Destination   **Ticket #**

Departure Time   **Arrival Time**

Airline: **Flight #**

Destination   **Ticket #**

Departure Time   **Arrival Time**

Passport #

(for international travel)

If necessary attach Medical Alert

What to Check on Before Your Flight

Airline seat reservations, advance seat selection and boarding passes

A relatively recent change in reservation operations is the ability to make your seat selection well before your flight. Each airline has its own time limit: some permit selection as long as 90 days in advance and others not until 30 days before your scheduled flight.

✔ Getting to the airport early used to guarantee getting a good seat. Today, with advance seat selection, this is no longer the case. In fact, advance selection is important for the reasons noted below.

● The most obvious reason is to avoid sitting in the uncomfortable middle seat of a three-seat row. If you make your selection early you can normally get a window or aisle seat. At the gate this may be impossible.

● If you are traveling with a partner, the best strategy to insure an empty seat next to you is for one of you to reserve the window seat and the other the aisle seat of the same row, toward the rear of the aircraft. This leaves the middle seat unreserved and these seats (especially those in the rear center rows) tend to be the last assigned.

● If you are traveling alone, ask the reservations agent to assign you a window or aisle seat in a row where another single is already assigned a window or aisle seat.

● On widebody aircraft, the rear center section is the last to fill up. If you ask for an aisle seat in the center section you will have the best chance of having an empty seat beside you.

● In case of an overbooked flight, anyone without a preassigned seat is treated virtually as a standby passenger. You will often have to wait until the last minute to board and are at the mercy of no-shows for available seats.

NOTE: Even if you have an advance boarding pass, it doesn't mean you can wander onto the plane only minutes before the flight. You must *still* let the airline personnel know you have arrived at the airport, so as not to be bumped or lose your reserved seat.

Most airlines will let preassigned seats go to standby passengers 10 minutes before departure. Some airlines have changed their policy to allow preassigned seats to be reassigned 20 minutes before departure. Know your airline's policy and adhere to it.

✔ Other seating considerations:

● If you do not like your preassigned seat, ask for a window, aisle or bulkhead seat when you check in at the airport. The airlines often do not release certain seats, such as bulkhead seats, until the day of the flight. If the ticket agent cannot help you, ask again at the gate. Gate personnel have much more immediate control of seating.

● Many airlines hold back the window and aisle seats in the front section of the coach section for their very-frequent flyers. These seats are not normally released until the day of the flight. The gate agent will be able to assign one of these unused seats if available just before departure.

● If you have an uncomfortable preassigned seat, check with airline personnel at the boarding gate.

They will release any unclaimed seats about 10 minutes before the flight and you normally can be reassigned an aisle or window seat. Some airlines release seats 20 minutes before departure.

● If you are already on the plane stuck in the middle seat or cramped next to an obese passenger, check out the airplane for any better empty seats. As soon as the passenger door closes, you may move to the better seat (in the same class of service) for a much more enjoyable flight. If you are on the first leg of a direct flight, you may have to move at the intermediate city if the seat has been assigned to a passenger boarding there.

● The safest seats on most aircraft are in the back third of the plane. According to articles based on recent published studies, the rear of the plane is up to 34 percent safer than the front, with the exception of some 727s with rear air-stair exits.

● Exit rows are often roomier, but often are not released until the day of the flight; children under age 15 are restricted from these seats as well as the handicapped. These seats also have additional restrictions which basically require that you can see and hear adequately and are physically able to open the emergency exits. (Exit row seats are also generally colder.)

● Avoid seats just in front of emergency exits—they do not recline much, if at all, so as to keep the exit clear in case of an emergency.

● Choose the aircraft you will be flying if possible. 727s, 737s and 757s are the most cramped. 767s, 777s, Airbuses and MD-80s are among the most comfortable. Some airlines offer greater pitch (distance between seats)—check with travel agents and friends or read *Consumer Reports Travel Letter* for a list of the roomiest airlines.

- Bulkhead seats sometimes have extra leg room and always eliminate the possibility of someone reclining their seat into your face. The trade-off may be a poor view of the movie, no permanent tray, and no storage area under the seat in front of you (everything has to go in overhead storage).

- Charter DC10s, L1011s and newer MD11s with 10-across seating are the worst. Avoid them.

- Think ahead about the sun's glare when selecting your seat. For instance: When flying early morning from north to south select a seat on the right-hand side of the plane (the west side); for flights south to north, do the opposite; east-west flights get glare from the south side of the plane (the left-hand side) and so forth.

- If you are a nonsmoker traveling on an international flight with a smoking section, you'll want to make sure you are not in the last rows of the nonsmoking area. People sitting in these rows are subjected to more intense secondhand smoke.

Airline meals

These are quickly becoming a relic of the past. Airline food service has been cut back, in most cases, to small snacks served on flights, longer than one-and-a-half hours that operate during normal meal hours.

We have all experienced airline food. We have all complained. Many of my frequent flyer friends—and parents traveling with children who are thinking ahead—always take their own cookies, snacks, fruits and cheeses to munch on during their flights. Others will only eat "special meals" detailed in the next section. Bottled water is often a good idea as well since it not only quenches thirst, but combats the dehydration caused by dry air in the aircraft cabin.

One of the most ironic twists to the airline meal saga has been the dramatic shift in passenger perception when it comes to eating during flights. For years, passengers complained that the food was terrible and that they didn't need so much to eat. The airlines listened. Now passengers complain that there is not enough to eat. Some even change flight plans to have an airline meal. Go figure.

Special meals

✔ Travelers can select special meals on many airlines. These must be ordered six to 24 hours, depending on the airline, before your flight departure. Any changes in your schedule will nullify your meal request. Special meals are not available on all flights or for all fares.

☛ KLM Royal Dutch Airlines offers 13 special meals in four categories—Diet, Religious, Vegetarian, and Children's. Their special selections include: • Diabetic • Low cholesterol/ low fat • Low calorie • Low sodium • High fiber • Kosher • Moslem • Hindu • Western vegetarian • Strict vegetarian • Asian vegetarian • Baby food and Child meals.

☛ Other airlines offer Gluten-free (no wheat, rye, barley, or oats), Bland (no seasoning), High protein, Lacto-vegetarian, Fruit, Seafood, Oriental, Kosher, Hamburgers, Peanut butter and jelly sandwiches, and sometimes even a birthday or wedding cake. United Airlines even offers Obento (a chilled Japanese meal) and McDonald's Friendly Skies Meals for children on some flights. USAirways has chicken legs and tater tots. Delta serves pizza.

Problems Enroute

Delayed & Canceled Flights

Airlines don't guarantee their schedules, and you should realize this when planning your trip. Many things can, and often do, make it impossible for flights to leave on time. Some problems, like bad weather and air traffic delays, are hard to predict and beyond the airlines' control. Others such as mechanical problems, flight crews failing to arrive on time or aircraft substitution may be within an airline's control.

This is an area that is not controlled by any laws. Each airline has its own policies under Rule 240. This rule generally states that under special circumstances such as a "schedule irregularity" or a "force majeure event," the airlines will make every effort to get passengers on to their final destination even if it means shifting the passenger to another carrier or upgrading their ticket.

NOTE: Rule 240 also states that if the airlines can not provide an onward flight "acceptable to the passenger," a refund can be issued—even for non-refundable airline tickets.

If your flight is delayed, try to find out why. But keep in mind that the airline employees may not have the answer. If the problem is with local weather or air traffic control, all flights will probably be late and there's not much you or the airline can do to speed up your departure.

If there's a mechanical problem with your plane, or if the crew is delayed on an incoming flight, you might be better off trying to arrange a flight on another airline. Ask the first airline to "endorse" (authorize the transfer of) your ticket to the new carrier; this should save you a fare increase. All major carriers have rules that allow agents to put delayed passengers on another carrier "at the request of the passenger."

When faced with a mechanical problem resulting in a delay, most airlines will attempt to keep their passengers traveling on their airline. Rather than transferring passengers to other carriers when faced with a delay, they either reroute passengers on another itinerary on their airline or simply ask them to wait. In many cases, waiting is the best and/or only option.

But in situations where competing airlines have flights traveling to the same destination, you may be able to have your ticket switched to another airline and arrive more or less on time. Many airlines follow a rule of thumb, I call the "four hour rule." If they can find transportation on their own aircraft that will allow the passenger to arrive within four hours of their originally scheduled arrival time, the airline may make travelers wait for the same airline's next flight heading to your destination. Once again, virtually every major airline's rule on delayed flights includes specific wording stating that onward transportation must be "acceptable to the passenger." This is where complaining and asking to be put on another airline will work (assuming there are flights with availability).

In some cases, normally encountered when traveling on some discount carriers, the airline accepting your "endorsed" ticket will require a "Flight Interruption Manifest" (FIM) as well.

If the flight is canceled, some airlines will re-book you at no additional charge on the first flight to your destination on which space is available. Finding space may be difficult, however, at holidays and peak travel times. Many airlines, if the cancellation was caused by other than an Act of God, will compensate you with a coupon for a free flight, similar to denied boarding compensation (see page 70), if you ask.

✔ **NOTE:** Rather than wait in a long line at the ticket counter or boarding gate for a seat reservation after an unexpected flight cancellation, call the toll-free reservations number and ask the agent to book you on the next available flight. That way you immediately lock in a new flight. You will only have to wait in line for the ticket change, but with great peace of mind.

Each airline has its own policies about what it will do for delayed passengers waiting at the airport. There is one constant rule—if you don't ask, the airlines won't give. Ask, ask, ask. Ask for a telephone call. Ask for a meal voucher. Ask to have your ticket be "endorsed" to another airline. Specific written amenity rules only concern when overnight accommodations are allowable. Any other amenities are strictly customer service.

If you are delayed, check with the airline staff to find out what services they will provide. Ask about meals and phone calls. Basically, if the delay is mechanical (the airline's fault) and for more than an hour they will go overboard to help; if the delay is due to weather (Act of God) you're on your own.

In cases where the airline decides to provide overnight accommodations for delayed passengers, remember that you are under no obligation to accept the lodging selected by the airline. If you are sent to a subpar motel or motor inn, you may complain and often be put up in a far better property.

Though the airlines will all vehemently deny it, passengers traveling with a full-fare coach ticket or full-fare Business Class or First Class will have more clout and often receive better compensation. Some of this treatment, such as easy endorsements to other airlines, is built into the fare structure. Sometimes the treatment, such as a free flight coupon or entry into the airline clubs, is based on the airline's interest in keeping a full-fare-paying passenger.

Some airlines, often those charging very low fares, do not provide any amenities to stranded passengers. Others may not offer amenities if the delay is caused by something beyond the airline's control.

Airlines almost always refuse to pay passengers for financial losses resulting from a delayed arrival. If the purpose of your trip is to close a lucrative business deal, to give a speech or lecture, to attend a family function, or to be present at any other time-sensitive event, you may want to allow a little extra leeway and take an earlier flight. In other words, airline delays and cancellations aren't unusual, and defensive counterplanning is a good idea when time is your most important consideration.

If you are holding a full-fare ticket, or any ticket for that matter, and you don't want to add to the confusion at the airport, but feel you should receive *some* compensation for a delay within the airline's control, write a letter to the airline's Customer Service Office. The addresses and phone numbers are listed in the back of this book.

AN IMPORTANT NOTE: Airlines are not responsible for getting passengers to the final destination on their itinerary if they were planning to change to another airline during their travels. For instance: a passenger flying on a shuttle flight from Boston to New York City may be delayed by air traffic (not unusual) and that delay causes the passenger to miss a connecting flight to Europe—the shuttle airline is not responsible for the passenger's failure to connect. Any additional fees to change tickets or costs of remaining in New York overnight will be the passenger's responsibility.

If the flights in question were connecting flights on the same airline or partner airlines, the policies of the airlines concerned would treat the passenger very differently and they would probably help make arrangements to get their passenger to Europe.

✔ Suggestions for anyone running late for a connection:

● If your flight is late and your connection at the next airport is in jeopardy, tell a flight attendant while you are in flight or let the gate agent know if you are still at the gate. Some airlines will make arrangements to take you by car or van between terminals, or use small electric carts that can get you to your gate much faster than you can get there walking. If there are enough late connecting passengers, airlines may delay connecting flights.

● While on the airplane, check the in-flight magazine for a diagram of the airport where you will be landing. The flight attendant can find out your arrival gate and that of your connecting flight. Knowing the layout of the airport can help you move a bit faster.

● As soon as you get off the plane let a customer service agent know about your problem. They often have radios or cellular phones and will call ahead to the gate to let the boarding personnel know you are on your way. The boarding crew also are in contact with the electric carts scooting between gates.

✔ Suggestions for anyone dealing with a predicted snowstorm or severe weather:

● If your flight turns out to be scheduled on the same day as a predicted snowstorm or other major weather problem, check with your airline to find out whether or not you can attempt to fly out on standby status the day *before* the snowstorm. Even if the telephone agent can't give you an answer, head to the airport. You'll find that, normally, most airline airport personnel are happy to get as many passengers out of their hair before the predicted cancellations and delays. I learned from one airline, operating from Boston before a predicted one-foot snowstorm, that all penalties and charges for changing all categories of tickets had been suspended for three days in order to ease the crunch at the airport during the storm.

If you can not get the airline to change your ticket on the phone, head to the airport. The gate agents have much more flexibility than any phone operator. If you still cannot get out on the day before a storm, head to the airport early on the day of your flight so that you have more opportunities to fly "standby" on an earlier flight. This way, you have a much better chance to take off before the airport closes or flights become hopelessly delayed.

✔ Suggestions for anyone changing a nonrefundable or special-fare ticket:

● Airlines often will allow you to change your ticket from one local airport to another without a charge. For instance, during your trip you may find that it is easier to fly to JFK rather than to Newark. If flights are "wide open," airlines may help out. Make these changes at the airline special services desk or at ticket offices, and there is normally no charge. However, make sure you have any arrangements in writing and your ticket is annotated properly *before* you head to the new departure airport. If you show up without a properly changed ticket, the airline may charge you the one-way fare back home.

● Never pay for anything at the airport thinking you can write a letter to the customer-service department and get your money back later. Once the airlines have your money, rarely will they return any. If you are told one thing by a telephone agent and another when you arrive at the airport, find a supervisor and sort out any confusion and necessary payments on the spot.

✔ **AIRPORT TIP:** If you have to spend the night at an airport at your own expense, see if the airline customer service representative will call and get a Distressed Passenger Rate for you, or ask the hotel manager (decision maker) for it yourself.

Dealing with Overbooking

Most airlines overbook their scheduled flights to a certain extent, and passengers are sometimes left behind or "bumped" as a result. There are two kinds of bumping: voluntary and involuntary.

Voluntary bumping

Almost any group of airline passengers includes some people with urgent travel needs and others who may be more concerned about the cost of their ticket than getting to a destination on time. Department of Transportation (DOT) rules require airlines to seek out people who are willing to give up their seats for some compensation before bumping anyone involuntarily.

Here's how this works: At the check-in or boarding area, airline employees will look for volunteers when it appears that the flight has been oversold. If you're not in a rush to arrive at your next destination, you can trade your time for money or its equivalent (normally a free ticket on a future flight).

But before you do this, you may want to get answers to these important questions:

● When is the next flight on which the airline can confirm your seat? The alternate flight may be just as acceptable to you. On the other hand, if they offer to put you on a wait-list or make you a standby on another flight that's full, you could be stranded.

● Will the airline provide other amenities such as free meals, hotel rooms, messages, phone calls, or transportation? If not, you may have to spend the money they offer you on food or lodging while you wait for the next flight.

The DOT has not said how much money the airline has to pay *volunteers*. This means airlines may negotiate with their passengers for an acceptable amount of money—or a free trip or other benefits. Airlines give employees guidelines for bargaining with passengers, and they may select those volunteers willing to sell back their seats for the lowest price.

Denied Boarding Compensation

The most prevalent form of compensation for passengers who are voluntarily bumped is a coupon, sometimes called a Denied Boarding Compensation (DBC) coupon, good for a round-trip flight anywhere within the airline's continental U.S. system (surprisingly, this includes Alaska with some airlines). But check for restrictions.

● These Denied Boarding Compensation coupons are normally good throughout the year, but some airlines may restrict their use during high-season blackout periods by requiring you to wait until the last day before issuing the ticket.

● Some DBC coupons are only for standby transportation.

● Some DBC coupons will result in First Class transportation. And many times the airlines will fly passengers who volunteered to be bumped First Class on the next flight, depending on availability.

● **Beware:** When you volunteer to be bumped and are held back from the flight, the flight crew may find a space once a physical passenger count is completed. In this case you will have to get back on your scheduled flight, but, perhaps, without your original seat. This rarely happens, but it has been reported.

Even with free tickets, many times you will hear the airline personnel upping the ante. If originally the airline needed 10 volunteers and only five passengers volunteered to be bumped, the gate personnel may offer cash as well. It is like an auction, and they seem to start at $200 plus the free ticket. The top price I have seen while a passenger was $500 and a free ticket, which resulted in almost half the plane volunteering. The first one to the airline representative got the deal. Naturally, everyone who had settled for no cash and only a free ticket, or less than $500, felt mistreated. As my brother says, "That's life on the Ponderosa."

Some flyers have made volunteering to be bumped a part of their check-in routine. As soon as they get to the gate, they ask if the flight is overbooked. If the answer is yes, they let the gate personnel know they are willing to volunteer. This places their name near the top of the list for bumping and getting a free ticket to anywhere in the airline's continental U.S. system. One Sunday after Thanksgiving, I managed three free tickets by successfully volunteering to be bumped from three flights in a row. If you have time, it means free transportation for you and makes life more pleasant for the airline personnel.

Involuntary bumping (U.S.)

Sometimes it doesn't even work to dangle escalating compensation for voluntary bumpees before a packed plane. If there aren't enough volunteers, some folk will be left behind *involuntarily*. This is where the law comes into play.

The DOT requires each airline to give all passengers who are bumped involuntarily a written statement describing their rights and explaining how the carrier decides who gets on an oversold flight and who doesn't. Those travelers who don't get to fly are frequently entitled to an on-the-spot payment. The amount depends on the price of their ticket and the length of the delay.

If you are bumped involuntarily and the airline arranges substitute transportation that is scheduled to get you to your destination (including later connections) within one hour of your original scheduled arrival time, there is no compensation. If the airline arranges substitute transportation that is scheduled to arrive at your destination more than one hour but less than two hours (four hours on international flights) after your original arrival time, the airline must pay you an amount equal to the one-way fare to your final destination, with a $200 maximum. If the substitute transportation is scheduled to get you to your destination more than two hours later (four hours internationally), or if the airline does not make any substitute travel arrangements for you, the compensation doubles (200 percent of the one-way fare, $400 maximum). You always get to keep your original ticket, and you can use it on another flight or have it refunded. The denied boarding compensation is a payment for your inconvenience.

Like all rules, however, there are a few important conditions and exceptions:

- To qualify for compensation, you must have a confirmed reservation, and you must have met the airline's deadline for buying your ticket.

- Each airline has a check-in deadline, which is the amount of time before scheduled departure that you must present yourself to the airline at the airport. The deadlines vary; it could be as little as 10 minutes, or longer than 90 minutes. Some airlines merely require you to be at the ticket/baggage counter by this time; others require that you get all the way to the boarding area. There is a separate ticketing deadline (usually at least 30 minutes before departure) for passengers picking up their tickets at the airport. If you miss the ticketing or check-in deadline, you may lose your reservation and your right to compensation if the flight is oversold.

● As noted above, no compensation is due if the airline arranges substitute transportation scheduled to arrive at your destination within one hour of your original arrival time.

● If the airline substitutes a smaller plane for the one it originally planned to use, the airline isn't required to pay people who are bumped as a result.

● The rules do not apply to charter flights, or to scheduled flights operated with planes that hold 60 or fewer passengers. They don't apply to international flights inbound to the United States, although some airlines on these routes follow them voluntarily. Also, if you are flying between two foreign cities—from Paris to Rome, for example—these rules will not apply (see next section on EC rules).

There are some steps you can take to minimize your chances of being bumped. When you book your reservations or buy your tickets, the agent can tell you what the airline's priorities are for honoring higher priced tickets before boarding people flying on discount fares. Most, however, bump the last people to arrive at the boarding gate. The most effective way to reduce the risk of being bumped is to get to the airport early.

Airlines may offer free transportation on future flights in place of money for denied boarding compensation. However, you have the right to insist on money if that is your preference. Once you take the money (or accept the free flight), you will probably lose the right to demand more money from the airline later on. However, if being bumped costs you more money than the

airline will pay you at the airport, you can try to negotiate a higher settlement with their complaint department. If this doesn't work, you usually have 30 days
from the date on the check to decide if you want to
accept the amount of the check. You are always free to
decline the check and take the airline to court to try to
obtain more compensation. A recent Supreme Court
ruling holds that federal airline regulations do not prevent bumped passengers from suing in state court to
recover their financial losses. The DOT's denied boarding regulation only spells out the airlines' *minimum*
obligation to people they bump involuntarily.

✔ **NOTE:** If you get bumped from a flight
anywhere other than in the U.S. and Europe,
these rules do not necessarily apply. Airlines
in some parts of the world offer more special
treatment while others offer you none.

Involuntary bumping
(European Union)

If your flight originates in the European Union and
you are bumped because of overbooking, you qualify
for immediate cash compensation no matter how
quickly the airline can get you to your destination. The
rules are based on the distance of your flight and the
length of time you will be delayed. (Compensation
listed in ECUs—European Currency Units—equal to
about US$1.10 at press time):

● For flights *less than 3,500 kilometers* (2,170
miles) with a resulting delay of two hours or
less from your scheduled flight you should

receive 75ECUs (about $83); if the delay is more than two hours you're due 150ECUs ($165).

● For flights *longer than 3,500 kilometers,* with arrival within four hours of your originally scheduled flight, you should receive 150ECUs (about $165); if your delay is more than four hours you get 300ECUs (about $330).

● Costs for phone or fax, normal meals you consume while waiting, and any lodging must also be paid by the airline.

● The airline may pay you with a voucher for future services, but if you prefer you will be paid with cash.

● Compensation will at no time be more than the price of your ticket. If you are traveling on a free ticket or with a charter, you are not entitled to any compensation.

Lost tickets

If you don't use an airline ticket for its original flight, you can usually change it. Most airlines will apply the fare printed on the ticket to another flight or itinerary.

Once upon a time, no one checked identification. Today that is not the case. But the airlines still treat lost tickets like currency. To an airline, your ticket is like currency: if you lose it, anyone who picks it up can take it to any airline and exchange it for transportation on a different flight—even to another city. Hence, replacing or refunding a lost ticket can be a major nuisance.

As a precaution, jot down the ticket number on a separate sheet of paper. Better, photocopy the ticket and put the copy in a place where you're not likely to lose it, or give it to a friend. With this information, if your ticket is lost, the airline can process your refund application more quickly, and perhaps issue an on-the-spot replacement.

America West, American, British Airways, Delta, Northwest, TWA, United and USAirways all require the ticket number for refunds. Southwest has no refund policy. British Airways has the most liberal policy with tickets reissued immediately when the ticket number is available for a $70 processing fee.

✔ Report a lost ticket immediately to the *airline* that issued the ticket. (If you bought the ticket from a travel agent or other outlet, the issuing airline is the one whose name was imprinted on the ticket.)

Once the airline establishes that you actually bought the ticket, they will process your refund application. Some airlines will do this right away, while others may wait up to six months. If anyone uses or cashes in your ticket while the refund is pending, the airline may refuse to give you your money back. Finally, there is a handling charge ($50-70) that the airline may deduct from the refund.

Many airlines, especially those that make passengers purchase tickets at the current fare (often the most expensive walk-up fare) will refund the lost ticket processing fee together with the original purchase price if the ticket is not used within 30 days to six months.

All in all, getting a refund or replacement for a lost ticket is a lot of trouble. And there's no guarantee you'll receive either with some airlines. So the best advice is—don't lose the ticket in the first place.

The new world of "ticketless travel" makes losing tickets a thing of the past if passengers are traveling ticketless. Your ticket is within the airline computer and can not be lost. It can only be claimed by the identifiable traveler assigned to the ticket.

The new I.D. checks that have been put in place to combat terrorist threats have also had a bonus effect of virtually eliminating the use of stolen tickets unless the tickets are stolen with a complete set of I.D. cards to back up identification.

Baggage handling and baggage problems

Between the time you check your luggage and the time you claim it at your destination, it may have passed through a maze of conveyor belts, baggage carts, and forklifts; when airborne, it may have tumbled around the cargo compartment in rough air. In all fairness to the airlines, however, relatively few bags are damaged or lost. With some common-sense packing and other precautions, your bags will probably be among the ones that arrive safely.

You can pack to avoid problems. Some items should never be put into the bag you check into the cargo system—money, jewelry, cameras, medicine, liquids, glass, negotiable securities, or any other things that are valuable, irreplaceable, delicate, or of sentimental value. These and anything else you absolutely need for your trip should be packed in a carry-on bag that will fit under the seat. Remember, the only way to be *sure* your valuables are not damaged or lost is to keep them with you.

Some seasoned travelers recommend carrying enough clothing and personal items with you in carry-on luggage to last 48 hours.

Baggage check-in time limits

This is a little-known rule, but it can be very important. All airlines have baggage check-in time limits which specify how long before a flight bags must be checked in order for the airline to be responsible for timely delivery of that baggage to its destination.

When the new baggage matching requirements go into effect, this rule becomes more important. Passengers will only be allowed to travel on the same plane with their baggage. This will make the baggage check-in limit the last moment passengers can arrive for a flight unless they can "gate check" their bags.

Delta has the most specific check-in deadlines—bags must be checked in 15 minutes before departure at most airports; 20 minutes before departure at Atlanta, New York JFK, Los Angeles, Orlando and Las Vegas; and 30 minutes before departure at Washington Dulles and Denver International Airport.

American, TWA and USAirways don't specify baggage check-in limits. They leave it up to the discretion of the agent. United has a 15-minute limit. Northwest has a 15-minute limit, except for Denver, where it is 25 minutes. Continental requires baggage check-in 20 minutes prior to a flight systemwide.

Late luggage waiver

If you arrive late for a flight, airlines often will want you to sign a Late Baggage Tag. Signing this ticket means that you accept all responsibility for the luggage not arriving at the same time you arrive. You will also be expected to pick up your luggage at the destination airport.

If you are running late for a flight your best bet is to carry your luggage with you to the gate and hand it to baggage handlers there. Many airlines will tag your bags at check-in so that you can just hand them to the gate personnel, this is called a "gate check."

Baggage limits and excess luggage charges

On domestic flights you are normally limited to a total of three pieces of luggage (this includes checked and carry-on bags). Again, this varies by airline.

The bags you check should be labeled—inside and out—with your name, address and phone number. Add the name and address of a person to contact at your destination if it's practical. Almost all bags misplaced by airlines do turn up sooner or later. With proper labeling, the bag and its owner can usually be reunited within a few hours.

Some airlines provide boxes for bulky items and garment bags. These boxes help bags arrive intact and are often free for the asking, but may also be available for a nominal fee.

Lock your bags to help prevent pilferage. Remove any shoulder straps and stow them inside, to prevent your bags from getting hung up in the baggage-handing machinery. But if your bags do arrive with broken locks or torn sides, check inside immediately. If something is missing, report it to the airline right away.

If you plan to check any electrical equipment, small appliances, typewriters, pottery, glassware, musical instruments or other fragile items, they should be packed in a container specifically designed to survive rough handling—preferably a factory-sealed carton or a padded hard-shell carrying case.

At check-in, the airline will put baggage destination tags on your luggage and give you the stubs to use as claim checks. Each tag has a three-letter airport code and flight number that show the baggage sorters to what airport and on which flight your luggage should go. Double-check the tag and flight number before your bags go down the conveyor belt. (The airline will be glad to tell you the code for your destination when you make reservations or buy your tickets, or at the check-in counter.) For a list of airline codes against which you can check your luggage tags when they are checked through go to one of these Web sites:

http://www.uni-karlsruhe.de/~un9v/atm/ase.html

http://www.bestfares.com/cyberlinks/airportcodes.htm

http://www.americanair.com/aa_home/servinfo/cityserv.htm

Remove all the previously attached baggage tags from your bag. They may confuse busy baggage handlers. Don't lose your claim checks—they are your only proof that you checked bags with the airline.

Make sure to ask about these situations:

● Some airlines you may be connecting on do not interline bags (transfer them between airlines). This normally affects Southwest, Reno Air and some other low-cost carriers as well as most charter flights.

● Some international flights require baggage to clear customs before your final destination. Local rules may require that you carry your own bag after customs to the transit counter for further connections.

Excess baggage charges can be a big surprise

Airlines use different methods for determining what is and is not excess, and then different calculations to come up with excess baggage charges.

American Airlines domestic excess baggage information: The limits are three pieces of baggage, whether checked or carried on the aircraft, with a maximum of two carry-ons (with two different specific maximum sizes). Its rules state that a briefcase, garment bag or collapsible luggage cart is considered part of the two-piece allotment. A carry-on pet, while not free, will count as the 45-inch carry-on.

Excess baggage charges are by bag rather than by weight. You can fill up each bag to a 70-pound maximum. The first three bags will cost $45 each; the next three, $65 each; and the seventh and additional bags will cost $130 each. The rules are thereafter based on whether the bags are oversized or weigh more than 70 pounds but less than 100 pounds, and so on . . .

Once the check-in agents decide that you have excess baggage, you can count on forking over a hefty supplement.

On flights in and from the U.S., airlines base excess baggage on a piece system, with a maximum of 70 pounds per piece. Between most other points, excess charges are based on weight.

Unusual baggage policies:

☞ Musical instruments, not exceeding 39 inches in length, may be transported in place of one of the bags included in free baggage allowance. If the instrument takes you over the three-bag limit or is longer than 39 inches, you must pay excess baggage charges. Large items such as a cello or bass fiddle may require purchase of an additional seat.

☞ Certain sports equipment may also be substituted for one of the free bags. The following qualifies:

Archery equipment, backpack, boogie board or knee board, bowling equipment (includes one ball, bag and one pair of shoes), fishing equipment (includes two rods, reel, net, tackle box and one pair of boots), golf equipment (one bag, 14 clubs, 12 balls and one pair of shoes contained in self-provided travel bag or box), hockey or lacrosse stick, shooting equipment, skateboard, ski equipment (one pair of skis, poles, boots and bindings), or snowboard. This equipment may exceed 62 inches in length with no oversize charges.

The following sports equipment always is subject to excess baggage charges:

Antlers, bicycle, empty scuba tank, surfboard, windsurfing and hang-gliding items.

Bicycles may be packed in a bag or box. American Airlines sells both bicycle boxes and bags. The bicycles are then sent for an additional $50 excess luggage charge. Most other airlines follow similar rules.

Certain aircraft (MD80 and 727 according to American Airlines) can not accept all oversized baggage. They provide a detailed dimension chart as do other airlines.

Hazardous items

Except for toiletries and medicines totaling no more than 75 ounces, it is illegal and extremely dangerous to carry on board or check in your luggage any of the following hazardous materials:

Aerosols—Polishes, waxes, degreasers, cleaners, etc.

Corrosives—Acids, cleaners, wet cell batteries, etc.

Flammables—Paints, thinners, lighter fluid, liquid reservoir lighters, cleaners, adhesives, camp stoves or portable gas equipment with fuel, etc.

Explosives—Fireworks, flares, signal devices, loaded firearms, gunpowder, etc. (Small arms ammunition for personal use may be transported in checked luggage securely packed in material designed for that purpose. These may not be placed in carry-on bags.)

Radioactives—Betascopes, radiopharmaceuticals, uninstalled pacemakers, etc.

Compressed gas—Tear gas or protective-type sprays, oxygen cylinders, divers' tanks (unless empty), etc.

Infectious substances, poisonous materials.

Matches (both strike anywhere' matches and safety or book matches) may only be carried on your person.

If you must travel with any of these materials, check with the airline's air freight department to see if special arrangements can be made.

A violation of the hazardous materials restrictions can result in a civil penalty of up to $25,000 for each violation or a criminal penalty of up to $500,000 and/or up to five years in jail.

Baggage limits in the U.S.A. vs. foreign limits

When traveling from the United States to a foreign country and then traveling by air on another flight later in your trip, be aware that baggage limits for trans-Atlantic flights on many airlines are simply based on the number of valises one checked onto the flight. When traveling within Asia or within Europe many airlines have much more restrictive limits.

According to the KLM and British Airways Web sites the baggage limit across the Atlantic is 32 kgs. (70 lbs.). The limit for intra-European flights for those flying tourist class is only 20 kgs. (44 lbs.) and for those flying business class it is 30 kgs. (66 lbs.). Some other regional airlines have even more stringent limitations.

Sending luggage ahead

One trick employed by seasoned travelers is to send their bulky items ahead by UPS, US Postal Service, Federal Express or other shipper. This allows you to avoid the hassles of lugging luggage. Just let the hotel, condominium office, or someone else at your destination know the package is being delivered and ask them to hold it until you arrive. On your return trip you can often call UPS or FedEx and they will pick up your box for its journey home.

✔ The shipping ahead method comes in especially handy when dealing with bulky children's items for a winter trip like snowsuits and snow boots. Some travelers ship mountain bikes and skis ahead. The added expense is often worth the ease of travel and peace of mind.

Carry-on baggage notes

According to the DOT there is no single federal standard for carry-on baggage, so check with the airline for any limits it places on the *size*, *weight* and *number* of carry-on bags.

● Inquire about your specific flights. The limitations vary depending on the type of aircraft.

● Check for each airline you are flying. Rules vary from one to another.

● Garment bag space is not unlimited, so some may have to be checked. Garment bags left in the front closet are not considered checked baggage.

● During holidays, especially the Sunday after Thanksgiving and the Sunday after Christmas, under-seat and above-seat capacity are pushed to their limits. Plan to carry less onto the plane with you and board early.

NOTE: There is no airline liability for lost carry-on baggage. If anything is lost, stolen or damaged it will be strictly your personal responsibility. However, some airlines will accept liability for carry-on luggage given to a flight attendent for storage.

✔ When considering what to take with you on a trip, note these things that are considered Free Personal Items:

Purse, laptop computer bag, overcoat, umbrella, reading material, infant necessities, canes, 35mm type camera (not including camera bag), binoculars, crutches, braces, collapsible walkers, unopened liquor less than 140 proof to be served by flight attendant, one golf club (that fits in overhead compartment), one infant seat or child restraint seat, a collapsible wheelchair or stroller or walker if non-collapsible, or 3-wheel models. Some airlines include a box of fish from Alaska and oranges from Florida in their free allowance.

When flying a commuter airline, there are additional limitations on carry-on baggage based on the size of the aircraft. In these cases those with carry-on luggage that is too big to bring onto the plane are allowed to "gate check" that luggage. It will be taken before boarding and will be set out next to the deplaning stairs where it may be picked up upon arrival without having to wait at the baggage carousel.

Baggage liability limits excess insurance

If your bags are lost or damaged on a domestic flight, the airline may invoke a $1,250 *per passenger* ceiling on the amount of money they'll pay you. (Legislation is pending to increase this liability to $1,850.)

When your luggage and its contents are worth more than that amount, check into Excess Valuation from the airline as you check in. This will increase the carrier's potential liability.

Excess Valuation Insurance is sold by most airlines for $1 to $2 for each $100 of coverage. There is normally a limit of $5,000 on this excess coverage. Check carefully to see exactly what the airlines do and do not cover, especially if you are traveling with a computer, art, antiques or other valuables.

The airline may refuse to sell excess valuation on some items that are especially valuable or breakable, such as antiques, musical instruments, jewelry, manuscripts, negotiable securities and cash. Whatever is not covered by the airline's insurance normally can be covered by your household goods insurance or a personal effects policy.

✔ **NOTE:** Your personal household goods or homeowner policy in most cases will cover items lost or damaged by the airlines (less any deductible).

Diners Club and American Express charge cards provide excess baggage insurance offering extra protection. See page 156 for more information or call your cardmember service number.

These policies vary greatly and rarely cover items such as computers or anything associated with your business. Business owners should carefully review their insurance policies to make sure that portable computers are insured against loss and damage. Also, anyone traveling with portable computers should keep backup disks separate from the computer.

Your claim must be supported by receipts. The airlines will only reimburse you for the depreciated value of items lost.

Some insurance professionals suggest you first submit any insurance claims against household insurance rather than against the airline. Your insurance company will then deal with the airline. This helps two ways—many policies cover replacement values (airlines never do) and your insurance company probably has more clout with the airlines than you do.

The Warsaw Convention Treaty and rules regarding checked luggage

On international trips, liability limits are set by the Warsaw Convention, a 1920s treaty regulating air commerce. Unless you buy excess valuation, the liability limits are 250 French gold francs per kilo (a kilo is about 2.2 pounds) of checked baggage, and the airlines have a formula for converting this limit into U.S. dollars. For example, as of press time, the limit was $9.07 per pound or $20 per kilo or about $640 *per bag* on international flights.

The Warsaw Convention also says that the airline must note your baggage weight on your airline ticket for you to take advantage of the liability limit. This way, if you file a claim, there will be a record of the weight on which to base the settlement. Some airlines write the total weight on the ticket at check-in time. Others explain in their notices that, if they lose or damage your luggage, they will assume that each checked bag weighs 32 kilos (70 pounds) for purposes of calculating that carrier's liability. In either case, it's a good idea to read the baggage notice on your ticket before you check your bags.

This international limit also applies to domestic segments of an international journey. This is the case even if the domestic and international flights are on separate tickets and you claim and recheck your bag between the two flights.

Keep in mind that the liability limits are maximums. If the depreciated value of your property is worth less than the liability limit, this lower amount is what you will be offered. If the airline's settlement doesn't fully reimburse your loss, check your homeowner's or renter's insurance; it sometimes covers losses away from the residence. Some credit card companies and travel agencies offer optional or even automatic supplemental baggage coverage.

Damaged bags

If your suitcase arrives smashed or torn, the airline will usually pay for repairs. If it can't be fixed, they will negotiate a settlement to pay you its depreciated value. The same holds true for clothing and items packed inside. Report external damage before you leave the airport. Insist on filling out a form.

Get the phone number for the *local* airline baggage services office. They are your best contact if you plan on having the bag repaired or replaced immediately.

Airlines may decline to pay for damage caused by the fragile nature of the broken item or your carelessness in packing. Airlines may also refuse to give you money for your damaged items inside the bag when there's no evidence of external damage to the suitcase, especially if it is soft-sided luggage. But airlines should not disclaim liability for fragile merchandise in the original factory sealed carton, a cardboard mailing tube, or other container designed for shipping and packed with protective padding material, or for goods packed in hard-sided luggage.

When you check in, airline personnel should let you know if they think your suitcase or package may not survive the trip intact. Before accepting a questionable item, they will ask you to sign a statement in which you agree to check it at your own risk. But even if you do sign this form, the airline should pay for damage caused by its own negligence, shown by external injury to the suitcase or package.

Delayed bags

If you and your suitcase don't connect at your destination, don't panic. The airlines have very sophisticated systems that track down about 98 percent of the bags they misplace and return them to their owners within hours.

If your bags don't come off the conveyor belt, report this to the airline *before* you leave the airport. You must fill out a form describing the bag, listing its contents (be as accurate as possible: this is the listing that any payments will be based upon), and providing other identification information for the baggage-tracing staff. Be sure to keep a copy of this form for your records.

To cover yourself have the airline fill out a form even if they say the bag will be on the next flight. Make sure to get the appropriate phone number for baggage service, not the reservations number. And get the name of the person who took the report.

Airlines will go to great lengths to deliver any delayed bags to you in your destination city at your home, hotel or other accommodation. The delay is usually only a few hours.

If the delay is longer, the airlines will generally absorb reasonable expenses you incur while they look for your missing belongings. You and the airline may have different ideas of what's reasonable, however, and the amount they will pay is subject to negotiation. Normally, the airlines consider basic clothing and toiletries as reasonable.

Most carriers set guidelines for their airport employees that allow them to disburse some money at the airport for emergency purchases. The amount depends on whether or not you're away from home and how long it takes to track down and return your bags.

These rules vary significantly from USAirways which provides no specifics, to Delta and United who acknowledge responsibility for delayed bags, to the Northwest rule that states the airline "will compensate the passenger for all reasonable, documented expenses incurred as a direct result of loss of, damage to, or delay in the delivery of any personal property."

If the airline does not give you a cash advance, be reasonable in what you buy if your bags are delayed. Purchase only necessities and keep all receipts.

If the airline misplaces sporting equipment such as skis or scuba equipment for use on a vacation, it will sometimes pay for the rental of replacements. For replacement clothing, the carrier may offer to absorb only a portion of the purchase cost, arguing that you will be able to use the new clothes in the future. However, they will often pay for rental clothing if you can locate a shop making such rentals.

When you've checked in fresh foods or any other perishable goods and they are ruined because their delivery is delayed, the airline won't reimburse you. Airlines may be liable if they lose or damage perishable items, but they won't accept responsibility for spoilage caused by temporary loss.

Airlines are liable for provable consequential damages (up to the $1,250 limit on domestic flights and $9.07 per pound limit on international flights, and whatever excess valuation you purchased) in connection with the delay. If you can't resolve the claim with the airline's airport staff, keep a record of the names of the employees with whom you dealt, and hold on to all travel documents and receipts for any money you spent in connection with the mishandling. (It's okay to surrender your baggage claim tags to the airline when you fill out a form at the airport, as long as you get a copy of the form and it notes that you gave up the tags.) Call or write the airline's consumer office when you get home. If you still do not get satisfaction from the airline, contact DOT (see page 170).

Lost luggage

Once your bag is declared officially lost, you will have to submit a claim. Some airlines will proceed using the form that you filled out when your bag was only thought to be delayed; others may require you to fill out a different form.

NOTE: Know the description of our luggage—the size, style, color, brand name and type of bag. Airline personnel and friends tell me it is amazing how many people can not identify their lost bags. One travel writer friend notes that some "admittedly paranoid" travelers have snapshots of their bags to give to agents in case the bags are lost.

✔ **Check on this:** failure to complete the second form when required could delay your claim. The airline will usually refer your claim form to a central office, and the negotiations between you and the airline will begin.

Airlines don't automatically pay the full amount of every claim they receive. They use the information on your form to estimate the value of your lost belongings, and like insurance companies, they consider the depreciated value of your possessions, not their replacement costs.

If you're tempted to exaggerate your claim, don't. Airlines may completely deny claims they feel are inflated or fraudulent. They often ask for sales receipts and other documentation to back up claims, especially if a large amount of money is involved. If you don't keep extensive records, you can expect to dicker with the airline over the value of your goods.

Generally, it takes an airline from six weeks to three months to pay you for your lost luggage. During this period, stay in touch with the company both to show your concern and to be sure they're following up on your claim. Even though the airlines lose relatively few bags, when they lose yours, you'll want to keep a watchful eye on the treatment of your claim.

When flying on an itinerary that includes several different airlines, it will be the final airline that will be responsible for handling your lost luggage claim. The investigation may prove that one of the other airlines was actually at fault, but all policies, rules and regulations of the last airline will be those passengers will have to follow.

NOTE: This makes a significant difference if the flight originated in the United States and landed in Europe after the passenger changed planes in New York. The lost luggage falls under international rules and the loss will be limited to $640 per piece of luggage rather than the $1,250 limit that would have been in effect had the bag been lost in the United States. This rule applies even if it is proven that the luggage was lost in the United States.

SMOKING RULES

Domestic flights

Under U.S. government rules, cigar and pipe smoking are banned on commercial aircraft. Smoking is prohibited on all domestic flights (including Puerto Rico and the Virgin Islands), except for flights to or from Alaska or Hawaii with a scheduled flight time of six hours or more.

Cigar and pipe smoking is banned on all U.S.-carrier flights (scheduled and charter, domestic and international).

International flights

Virtually all U.S. airlines and many foreign carriers have created smoke-free international flights or have banned smoking completely. Each airline will let passengers know whether the flight they have selected is nonsmoking.

Smoking is also banned on other scheduled-service flights by U.S. airlines that are operated with planes seating fewer than 30 passengers (e.g., certain commuter flights to Canada, Mexico and the Caribbean).

These following rules apply to cigarette smoking when permitted on U.S. airlines flying internationally—both scheduled and charter.

● The airline must provide a seat in a nonsmoking section to every passenger who asks for one, as long as the passenger complies with the carrier's seat assignment deadline and procedures. (Therefore, standby passengers do not have this right.)

● If necessary, the airline must expand the non-smoking section to accommodate the passengers described above.

● The airline does not have to provide you a nonsmoking seat with your traveling companion, and you don't have the right to specify a window or aisle nonsmoking seat.

● Smoke drifting from the smoking section into the nonsmoking section is not a violation.

● No smoking is allowed while an aircraft is on the ground or when the ventilation system is not fully functioning.

● **Never smoke in airplane restrooms.**

Smoking was banned in all but the designated smoking sections after 116 people were killed in only four minutes, apparently because a smoker left a burning cigarette butt in the trash bin.

● **Don't smoke while standing.**

In case of air turbulence your cigarette may end up burning someone (expect a liability suit) or starting a fire.

▲ FYI: Foreign airlines flying internationally don't have to follow these rules, but most of them offer nonsmoking sections anyway. About three dozen countries now ban smoking on all or some domestic flights. Almost a third of these countries are in Europe. If avoiding smoke is important to you, ask the airlines about their smoking policies.

On-board Health

Considerations

✈ **Dehydration**: Aircraft cabin air is about the driest we experience. To combat dehydration, which often causes headaches, coughing, itchy skin and sore eyes, drink a glass of water every hour. Also try to avoid drinking alcoholic beverages and eating salty snacks—they increase dehydration. (Coffee, tea, and such caffeinated soft drinks as Coke and Pepsi also promote dehydration.)

If you request water, ask for bottled water or mineral water. The water tanks on most planes are not regularly drained and refilled with fresh water. In most planes these water tanks are just topped off, so water can seem stale.

Some seasoned business travelers carry bottles of spring water with them since there is very limited service on most flights in coach.

✈ Don't wear contact lenses—they are normally very uncomfortable in super-dry air. If you must wear contacts, bring plenty of rewetting solution. Airliner air is dry; if you wear contact lenses, blink often and limit reading.

Alcohol and coffee both have a drying effect on the body. Airliner cabin air is relatively dry to begin with, and the combination can increase your chances of contracting a respiratory infection. If you wear contact lenses, the low cabin humidity and/or consumption of alcohol or coffee can reduce your tear volume, leading to discomfort if you don't blink often enough. Lens wearers should clean their lenses thoroughly before the flight, use lubricating eye drops during the flight, read in intervals, and take the lenses out if they nap. (This may not apply to extended wear lenses; consult your practitioner.)

✈ **Recycled air**: This has caused much discussion, but recent studies show that the airlines' policy of limited recycling of air has no measurable effect on passengers' health.

✈ **Traveling with a cold:** This is not a good idea, but sometimes inevitable. Take a decongestant about an hour before takeoff and again 45 minutes before landing to help ease ear blockage and sinus agony.

✈ If you take prescription medications, bring enough to last through your trip. Take along a copy of the prescription, or your doctor's name and telephone number, in case the medication is lost or stolen. The medicine should be in the original prescription bottle in order to avoid questions at security or Customs inspections. Carry it in a pocket or a carry-on bag; don't pack it in a checked bag, in case the bag is lost.

Pressure changes

Flying is a routine activity for millions of Americans, and raises no health considerations for the great majority of them. However, there are certain things you can do to ensure that your flight is as comfortable as possible.

Changes in pressure can temporarily block the eustachian tube, causing your ears to pop or to experience a sensation of fullness. To equalize the pressure, swallow frequently; chewing gum sometimes helps. Yawning is also effective. Avoid sleeping during descent; you may not swallow often enough to keep ahead of the pressure change.

If yawning or swallowing doesn't help, use the valsalva maneuver: Pinch your nostrils shut, then breathe in a mouthful of air. Using only your cheek and throat muscles, force air into the back of your nose as if you were trying to blow your thumb and finger off your nostrils. Be very gentle and blow in short successive attempts. When you hear or feel a pop in your ears, you have succeeded. Never force air from your lungs or abdomen (diaphragm); this can create pressures that are too intense.

Babies are especially troubled by these pressure changes during descent. Having them feed from a bottle or suck on a pacifier will often provide relief.

Avoid flying if you have recently had abdominal, eye or oral surgery, including a root canal. The pressure changes that occur during climb and descent can result in discomfort.

A final tip on pressure changes: they cause your feet to swell. Don't wear new or tight shoes while flying.

Passengers with disabilities

Over 40 million Americans have disabilities. The Air Carrier Access Act and the DOT rule that implements it set out procedures designed to ensure that these individuals have the same opportunity as anyone else to enjoy a pleasant flight. Here are some of the major provisions of the rule.

A person may not be refused transportation on the basis of disability or be required to have an attendant or produce a medical certificate, except in certain limited circumstances specified in the rule.

Airlines must provide enplaning, deplaning and connecting assistance, including both personnel and equipment. (Some small commuter aircraft may not be accessible to passengers with severe mobility impairments. When making plans to fly to small cities, such passengers should check on the aircraft type and its accessibility.)

Airport terminals and airline reservations centers must have TDD telephone devices for persons with hearing or speech impairments.

Passengers with vision or hearing impairments must have timely access to the same information given to other passengers at the airport or on the plane concerning gate assignments, delayed flights, safety, and so on.

New widebody aircraft must have a wheelchair- accessible lavatory and an on-board wheelchair. Airlines must put an on-board wheelchair on most other flights upon a passenger's request (48 hours' notice required).

Air carriers must accept wheelchairs as checked baggage, and cannot require passengers to sign liability waivers for them (except for preexisting damage).

Most new airplanes must have movable armrests on half the aisle seats, and on-board stowage for one folding passenger wheelchair.

Carriers must allow service animals to accompany passengers in the cabin, as long as they don't block the aisle or other emergency evacuation route.

FAA safety rules establish standards for passengers allowed to sit in emergency exit rows; such persons must be able to perform certain evacuation-related functions.

FAA rules also prohibit passengers from bringing their own oxygen. Most airlines will provide aircraft-approved oxygen for a fee, but aren't required to.

Airlines may not charge for services that are required by this rule.

Airlines must make available a specially-trained Complaints Resolution Official if a dispute arises. There must be a copy of the DOT rule at every airport.

It's wise to call the airline again before your trip to reconfirm any assistance that you have requested. For additional details, order the booklet *New Horizons for the Air Traveler with a Disability* from the Government Printing Office.

Frequent-flyer programs

Virtually all major U.S. airlines have a frequent-flyer plan, and many foreign carriers are starting them. These programs allow you to earn free trips, upgrades (e.g., from Coach to First Class) or other awards based on how often you fly on that airline. In some programs you can earn credit by using specified hotels, rental car companies, credit cards, etc.

It doesn't cost anything to join a program, and you can enroll in the programs of any number of different airlines. However, it may not be to your advantage to put all your eggs in one basket with one plan by accumulating a high mileage balance only to find out later that another carrier's program suits your needs better.

Here are some things to look for when selecting a frequent-flyer program.

- Does the airline fly where you want to go?

- Are there tie-ins with other carriers, especially those with international routes? Is some of the airline's service provided by commuter-carrier partners? In both cases, can you earn credits and use awards on those other airlines?

- How many miles (or trips) are required for particular awards?

- Is there a minimum award per flight (e.g., you are only flying 200 miles but the airline always awards at least 500)?

- Is there a deadline for using accumulated miles?

- Carefully examine the number and length of any blackout periods during which awards cannot be used. On some carriers, the Thanksgiving blackout may last a week.

- If you are planning a big trip and are thinking about joining that airline's frequent-flyer program, enroll before you travel. Airlines usually won't credit mileage that was flown before you became a member.

After you join a program, there are other things that you should know:

- Is there a deadline for using accumulated miles?

- Airlines reserve the right to make changes to their programs, sometimes on short notice. The number of miles required for particular awards might be raised, requiring you to use your old mileage (i.e., your current balance) under the more restrictive new rules. The airline may cease service on a route that you were particularly interested in or it may drop the city you live in! The carrier may eliminate attractive frequent-flyer tie-ins with particular airlines or hotel chains.

- Carriers often limit the number of seats on each flight for which frequent-flyer awards can be used. You may not be able to get reservations on your first- or second-choice dates or flights. However, once a frequent flyer ticket is issued, it can be used for standby travel at any time. If flyers learn the ins and outs of standby travel, this is where it will serve them well.

- Awards can often be issued in the name of immediate family members. However, if you sell or give an award to someone not named on the award or the travel document and the airline finds out, the recipient could have his or her ticket confiscated, and the carrier may penalize the program member's account balance.

- Ask the airline how mileage is registered; you will probably have to identify yourself as a program member when you book your flight or when you check in.

- Keep your boarding passes and the passenger coupon of your ticket until you receive a statement from the frequent-flyer program reflecting the correct mileage earnings for that trip. If a problem arises, get the names of the people you speak with and keep notes of your conversations.

NOTE: Remember that normally your frequent flyer benefits are considered part of your estate. Most award mileage will be transferred to the heir's account or handled according to the will. Once again, the rules vary between airline frequent flyer programs, but most programs have a way of dealing with accrued mileage as an asset of an estate.

In some cases, unused frequent flyer mileage can be donated to charity as well as to friends and family. Check with your program to get applicable details.

Warsaw Convention Treaty Death Liability Limits

Surprisingly, many aspects of the airline industry are still governed by the Warsaw Convention which was ratified before World War II. This agreement covers among other things, airline monetary liability limits for damages for death or injury to passengers and liability for damages caused by lost or damaged luggage.

The Warsaw Convention only comes into effect when flying internationally. It has remained unchanged for decades. Domestic flights within a country are not covered by this convention.

We have already covered the liability limits for luggage. A proposed change to the death and injury liability limit is currently in the process of being ratified. The limited liability is, under the Warsaw Convention, $75,000 per passenger for death or injury. However, an intercarrier agreement has been signed by about 90 of the world's airlines which will voluntarily eliminate any liability limit should the airlines be found negligent and impose a new limit of approximately $145,000, which comes into effect only if the airline can prove that it was not negligent.

Under the current Warsaw Convention Treaty, claimants must prove that the airline was negligent before they can collect even the $75,000. The new ground rules created by the interairline agreement allow passengers (or their families and heirs) to make their claims against the airline even without a finding of negligence.

Auto Rights

The simple part of automobile rentals is the basics—you need a valid driver's license and a credit card. But, what many once took for granted—multiple drivers, inclusive liability insurance, and the ability to rent a car as long as you had a valid driver's license—has changed and is not always part of the rental agreement.

> **NOTE:** Debit cards, even with the MasterCard or Visa logo, will not be accepted by rental car companies at time of rental. They may be used for payment upon return of the vehicle.

What most travelers know was not ever included in rental agreements, such as collision damage waiver, now can be included—to a greater or lesser extent—if certain credit cards are used to rent certain types of cars in certain circumstances for a certain length of time and when driven along certain types of roads.

None of this seems complex until you end up in an accident or have to modify a reservation at the last minute. Or until you are faced with a rental agent who looks you straight in the eye and tells you your credit card collision damage waiver (CDW) doesn't cover the automobile you are planning to rent. (At least he or she "can't guarantee that the car is covered" or they "wouldn't want to chance it.")

Naturally, none of us wants to "chance it" with massive liabilities. If you have any questions, simply pick up the phone and call your credit card company. All have special numbers to call for collision damage waiver information. The 800 number on your card will allow you to reach those experts so you can be sure. The next pages show how much these policies vary. So read on and be prepared before you face the agents.

Collision damage waiver

In this section, we deal with the most common source of confusion for automobile renters—collision damage waiver (CDW) or loss damage waiver (LDW). There are several basics:

❑ Most people who rent automobiles do not need to pay for the additional collision damage waiver. They have other coverage which, in effect, duplicates the expensive rental car company waiver.

❑ If you have your own automobile insurance with collision coverage, you probably have enough liability insurance to meet most legal challenges and most small collisions. However, most personal automobile policies limit the amount of damages paid to the value of your *personal* car. Check with your insurance company to find out exactly what their coverage is on rental cars.

❑ Most Visa Gold and Gold MasterCard credit cards, some normal credit cards, Diners Club and American Express provide a form of CDW.

❑ Credit cards provide one of two types of coverage—

Primary coverage means that while you are renting a car according to the card rules, the credit card waiver is your primary insurance. If you have an accident, your own insurance will not be responsible for any payments.

Secondary coverage (the most prevalent form) means that in case of an accident your own automobile insurance company is responsible for initial insurance payments and the credit card will pay any excess not covered by your personal auto insurance.

How credit card CDW works

The collision damage waiver you get with your credit card is not the same as purchasing CDW from the rental company.

The rental company CDW releases you from any responsibility for damage to the vehicle in case of accident. With credit card CDW you are personally responsible for any damages: in some cases you must pay the car-rental company for the damages and will be reimbursed by your credit card company. In other situations the credit card company will pay the damages directly to the car-rental company—they are paying your bill.

If, in case of an accident, you cannot afford to make a short-term damage payment until you are reimbursed by your personal automobile insurance and the credit card company, you may be better off paying for the CDW sold by the rental-car company.

Once you know what your insurance covers and you decide to use your credit card collision waiver, you activate the waiver by charging the rental against your credit card and declining all waivers or insurance offered by the rental car company.

The basic credit card coverage will include physical damage to the car, theft of the car, towing charges and a "loss-of-use" charge.

In an actual incident my rental car windshield was cracked by a rock thrown up by a truck while crossing a mountain pass in Colorado. Dollar noted that my rental was paid for with a Diners Club credit card. I called Diners Club and reported the incident. They sent me all necessary forms and paid for the broken windshield and the day or so of "lost usage" claimed by Dollar. Though there was paperwork involved, it was minimal. The system worked smoothly and efficiently.

When you have an accident with a rental car and your coverage is with your own insurance and the credit card CDW, make sure to make all your reports in a timely manner. Credit cards have strict claims reporting deadlines.

NOTE: Credit card company policies vary significantly, not only in their primary and secondary coverage, but also in length of rental that is insured. The basic rule seems to be that automobile rentals here in the U.S. are covered up to 15 days. Foreign rentals are covered for 15 to 31 days, so make sure your collision damage waiver will last as long as your planned rental.

☞ If you use a Diners Club card you are covered worldwide with full value primary insurance for 31 days.

☞ Some American Express cards provide secondary coverage for up to 30 days; normal Optima cards (except the Delta Optima Card) do not provide CDW.

☞ MasterCard BusinessCard provides full-value primary collision/loss damage insurance, but only for 15 days.

☞ MasterCard Gold provides secondary insurance for 15 days (international rentals get primary insurance).

☞ Visa Gold provides secondary coverage for 15 days domestically and primary coverage for 31 days internationally.

Some airline and travel program affinity credit cards issued by Visa and MasterCard provide CDW. But, as of 1997, Continental, TWA, Midwest Express, Southwest and United's standard cards did not include this.

Almost every other normal Visa and MasterCard does not include CDW coverage. Discover Card does not provide collision damage waiver. Of the American Express Optima Cards, only the Delta affinity card and the Platinum version provide CDW.

Credit card CDW programs

❏ As noted above, most credit cards provide secondary insurance coverage. Several charge cards offer primary coverage, but their numbers are dwindling. Check the fine print in your card agreement to find out what type of coverage your card provides.

❏ Diners Club and MasterCard BusinessCard are the only cards that offers full-value primary insurance to all card holders for domestic and international rentals. Recently Visa has also announced a business card with primary insurance.

❏ Check carefully to find out whether the CDW provided by your credit card will cover additional drivers listed on the rental contract. Also see whether the credit cards provide loss of revenue coverage, which reimburses the rental car company for any revenue lost while the car is being repaired.

❏ Check with your credit card issuer to find out which automobile models are covered by their policy.

> **Note: There are many differences in credit-card collision damage coverage.**

Credit card CDW provides a lesson in the importance of reading the fine print. Though credit card companies never talk about the differences in their rental collision policies, they can make a big difference in deciding which card to use.

❏ If you are renting a Mercedes or BMW in the U.S. you'll have to use the AT&T Visa Gold or Diners Club; the other cards don't provide coverage.

❏ If you are planning a trip in a minivan and don't know which make of vehicle you'll get from the rental company, use Diners Club or AT&T Gold MasterCard—all minivans are covered.

❏ If you are going to rent a sport/utility vehicle such as a Jeep Wrangler, Jeep Cherokee, Chevrolet Blazer, Ford Bronco or Suzuki Samurai and plan to drive it only on paved roads, use the American Express Card, Diners Club or Visa Gold—they give complete coverage. MasterCard Gold specifically excludes them.

Credit card coverage specifics

 CitiBank MasterCard BusinessCard does not cover:

"Rental of trucks, campers, Jeep-type vehicles, trailers, off-road vehicles, motorbikes, recreational vehicles, vans or minivans mounted on a truck chassis (call the MasterCard Assistance Center before renting a van or minivan to confirm whether the vehicle is covered), antique cars (which means cars that are over 20 years old or have not been manufactured for 10 or more years), limousines, expensive or exotic cars (for example, Corvette, Mercedes Benz, Porsche, Jaguar; call the MasterCard Assistance Center before renting a car to confirm whether the vehicle is covered); except that restrictions on exotic or expensive cars do not apply to cars rented outside the United States."

American Express Corporate Card does not cover the following vehicles:

Expensive cars, valued at over $50,000 (restrictions on expensive, exotic or antique cars do not apply to cars rented outside the U.S., its territories and possessions).

- Exotic cars, such as Aston-Martin, Bentley, Bricklin, Cadillac Fleetwood Limo, Daimler, DeLorean, Excalibur, Ferrari, Jensen, Lamborghini, Lincoln Limo, Rolls-Royce, Porsche, or similar vehicle;

- Antique cars (over 20 years old or not manufactured for 10 or more years);

- Off-road vehicles, motorcycles, mopeds, recreational vehicles, trucks, campers, trailers, certain vans, and any other vehicle which is not a rental car;

- Minivans which are used for commercial hire. (Minivans are covered when rented for personal and business use only.)

- Four-wheel drive sport/utility vehicles when driven off-road. (Four-wheel drive vehicles, including but not limited to Jeep Wrangler, Jeep Cherokee, Chevrolet Blazer, Ford Bronco and Suzuki Samurai, are covered when driven on paved roads.)

- Cars rented in Jamaica, Ireland, Israel, Italy, Australia and New Zealand.

 MasterCard Gold and Platinum Cards have the same MasterRental® program.

- According to material taken from the MasterCard Web site most vehicles are covered, including all minivans.

- Excluded rental vehicles: Trucks, sport utility vehicles (e.g., Jeep Cherokee), full-size vans mounted on truck chassis, campers, off-road vehicles (e.g., Jeep Wrangler) and other recreational vehicles, trailers, motorbikes, antique cars (which means cars that are over 20 years old or have not been manufactured for at least 10 years), limousines, expensive or exotic cars, (e.g., Corvette, Mercedes Benz, Porsche, Jaguar). If you have any questions, or to confirm coverage for a particular vehicle, call 1-800-MC-ASSIST.

- Restrictions on expensive or exotic cars do not apply to rentals outside the U.S.

 Visa Gold Auto Rental Insurance excludes the following vehicles on a worldwide basis:

- Expensive, exotic, and antique automobiles; certain vans; trucks; motorcycles, mopeds, and motorbikes; limousines; and recreational vehicles.

- Examples of excluded expensive or exotic automobiles are the Aston-Martin, Bentley, Bricklin, Daimler, DeLorean, Excalibur, Ferrari, Jensen, Lamborghini, Lotus, Maserati, Porsche, and Rolls-Royce. However, BMW, Mercedes-Benz, Cadillac, and Lincoln are covered worldwide (as long as they are not models otherwise excluded).

- An antique automobile is defined as any vehicle over 20 years old or any vehicle that has not been manufactured for 10 years or more.

- Only vans that are standard vehicles with standard equipment and designed to carry a maximum of eight people are covered.

- If you have any questions, or to confirm coverage for a particular vehicle, call 1-800-VISA-911.

Other credit card insurance limitations

❑ Your credit card collision damage waiver does not cover any damage to the *other* car. The American Express Corporate Card Description of Coverage states, "For example in the event of a collision involving the Cardmember's rental car, damage to the other driver's car or the injury of anyone or anything are not covered."

❑ If you get into an accident and it can be proved that you were intoxicated (with drugs *or* alcohol), many credit card collision damage policies, such as the American Express, Diners Club, and those of AT&T Universal Card, will not pay any claims. The MasterCard BusinessCard policy doesn't mention that factor.

❑ Remember the claims reporting requirements when using credit card CDW and personal insurance. You are responsible for all the follow-up. Diners Club has a 90-day claims reporting limit, but Visa and MasterCard are much more limited.

Visa rules require that the accident and claim be reported to Visa within 20 days of the date of loss; then the Visa Auto Rental Claim form must be completed and postmarked within 90 days of the loss whether or not the supporting materials have been gathered.

MasterCard rules are not as stringent. Claims must be reported within 30 days. You will be sent a claims form which must be completed and sent in with other required documentation.

American Express requires the first report within 48 hours. They will send a claims form to be returned with supporting documents within 60 days (Amex allows additional time for the final claim).

Liability coverage

Although collision damage is limited to the value of a vehicle you might total, liability for personal injury is virtually unlimited and therefore much more significant. Unfortunately, the laws covering personal injury are as varied as the states. Everything—vehicle ownership, driver negligence, mechanical failure, and more—comes into play. There are no absolutes, except that you should make sure you are covered in some way.

Once upon a time, full, primary liability insurance was included in all car-rental contracts, but that has changed. Today, in most states, most of the largest car rental companies only provide secondary liability coverage. That is, they pick up your coverage when your personal insurance is exhausted.

This pattern is spreading. Take time to find out what liability coverage is provided when you make your reservations and be ready to make sure you have adequate liability coverage.

Liability/collision insurance limitations on personal automobile policies

On the personal automobile insurance side of the question, some insurance companies are now starting to eliminate the automatic inclusion of collision and liability coverage for policy holders who travel on business. In the case of personal rentals many companies are making their liability coverage secondary.

Make sure to check your policy carefully. Coverage varies on a state-by-state basis. This additional rental car coverage for business travel is often available only as an optional rider.

Negotiating rental car rates

Rental car rates are as complicated as airline rates. In addition to daily, weekly, weekend, subcompact, compact, mid-sized, and so forth, renters have to deal with frequent-flyer rates, automobile club rates, and other special promotional rates. If you don't already have a good idea of what rate you want to pay, your chances of getting the lowest rate are significantly diminished.

Most automobile rental agents can not inform potential renters of the lowest rates available unless prompted by references to specific promotional rates quoted from newspapers or frequent-flyer brochures. To be honest, with such a complicated matrix of prices, the rental agents simply have no idea of the "best" rate until they learn which associations, frequent flyer clubs, insurance programs, travel clubs and so on to which you belong.

> ✔ With rental car rates, research is as important as with airline tickets, even more so—airline reservationists will almost always offer the lowest rate on a given flight on a specific day. Rental car reservationists must be carefully prompted to get the lowest rate. Many times even they do not know which combination of association discount, frequent flyer program and rental contract will result in the lowest rental rate.

Large associations like USAA and AAA have negotiated rates which are a bargain if you must rent a car on short notice during the week. However, these negotiated rates are not as big a bargain as many of the promotional and weekend rates car rental ads tout.

Often the best rates are through airline frequent-flyer programs or associated with the airline upon which you arrive at the airport where you pick up your car.

Reservationists have told me that great deals are available to members of wholesale clubs such as Sam's or Price/COSTCO.

Once you have made a reservation for a specific car at a specific rate, the rental car company is committed to providing you that rate, but not necessarily that size car. For example, if after making a reservation for a compact, you arrive and no compacts are available, the rental car company must provide you another car of the same or greater size for the same rate. If only smaller cars are available, the rental car company should make that car available at a reduced rate based on your *original* rental rate.

Again, everything is up for negotiation and depends to a large degree on the manager on duty and your bargaining skills.

If you have rented a car for a fixed number of days, many major car rental agencies require that you keep your car for a minimum number of days. Incidents have been reported where renters returning automobiles early have been charged the normal daily rate rather than the pre-negotiated weekly rate. This may result, in some cases, to a doubling of the daily rate. For your own protection, when you make your reservation, ask whether returning the car early means paying a different rate.

Non-U.S. residents planning to rent automobiles in the United States should call ahead for special weekly rental rates before leaving their home country. Often travelers can garner significant savings by signing up for one of the tourism rates major rental companies offer foreign tourists.

Cancellation fees

Check whether your automobile reservation is subject to a cancellation fee. These fees are not widespread, but they are creeping into the automobile rental industry. They are found in major vacation destinations such as Florida, Southern California and Hawaii.

The normal charge is $25. Our basic rule is not to make any reservation that may result in a cancellation fee. If the deal is so extraordinary that you are willing to be liable for this fee, go ahead. But if you have to cancel the reservation, make sure to get the cancellation number and the name of the agent with whom you speak.

Mileage caps and additional mileage charges

Always ask whether your car rental is with unlimited mileage or whether there is a limit to free miles. Many rental car companies provide their automobiles for rent with a limit on the mileage included in the quoted rate. In many cities mileage quickly adds up and when driving even relatively modest distances, you'll be surprised how quickly miles roll by. When automobile rental companies place a limit on mileage, they charge anywhere from 20¢ to 25¢ per additional mile—that adds up fast.

Geographical restrictions

Some rental car companies will only allow their automobiles to be driven within the state in which the car was rented or some other limited geographic region.

Always ask whether there are geographic limitations on the automobile rental. This is very important in border locations where renters might assume they can drive the automobile into Canada or Mexico and it most often is not the case. (See page 130.) This also comes into play when considering rentals in Europe where travel in the former Eastern Bloc countries is planned. Make sure the rental car you are picking up can be driven in to Eastern Europe. (See page 133.)

Some rental car companies also have restrictions on the types of cars permitted to be driven into Italy. Many times Mercedes and BMWs may not be taken into Italy. Check before you leave the counter. These policies are in place because of the high rate of automobile theft in those locations. For instance, one report I recently received indicated that one out of eight automobiles rented in Naples, Italy, is never returned.

If a rental car disappears while it is in a restricted country, the drivers are out of luck and the insurance, whether with your credit card or directly from the rental car company, will not normally apply.

Additional driver rules and charges

❏ Many rental car companies now charge up to an additional $15 per additional driver *per day*. If you are renting a car and plan to share the driving, make sure to check out additional driver charges. They can come as a surprise at the car rental counter, and can ruin what appeared to be a good deal.

❏ These additional driver charges vary greatly between rental locations. Some Hertz, Avis, Alamo, Dollar, Payless, Thrifty and other locations charge nothing for additional drivers; other charge $3.50 per rental and yet others assess anywhere from $4 up to $10 per day. Hertz waives additional driver charges for all AAA members. Some locations charge for additional drivers under 25 years of age but don't charge for other additional drivers. Some rental companies charge for spouses and family members, others don't.

❑ Some rental car companies exempt drivers on business or government workers traveling officially.

NOTE: When you rent a car, every additional driver must be on the rental form or it must be clearly stated that "immediate family members may drive the automobile" or something to that effect. If not, any collision damage or liability insurance is null and void in case of an accident by a driver not recorded on the form.

Charges for younger drivers

Most automobile rental companies require drivers to be at least 25 years of age and have a major credit card. Some companies have a lower age limit of 21 with an additional charge for those ages 21 to 24.

Alamo, Dollar, Payless and Thrifty seem to have the most liberal rental policies for drivers aged 21–24. For the most part, they assess a $20 per day surcharge.

One-way rentals

Renting a car at one location and then dropping it off at another location usually results in additional charges. In some cases, rental car companies will allow renters to pick up a car at one regional airport and then drop the car off at another airport or downtown location in the same region. This may be the case in San Francisco where there are two major airports as well as numerous downtown locations. It may also be possible in the Los Angeles region where nearby airports such as Ontario and LAX may be treated by some rental car companies as the same region so they waive drop-off charges. However, always ask about drop-off charges whenever you rent a car and will be dropping it off at another location, even when the drop-off location may be only a few miles away.

Some rental car companies have weekly rates or slightly higher daily rates for rentals that will be dropped off in the same state or between specific high-traffic city pairs such as Chicago-St. Louis or Washington D.C.-Boston. The bottom line is call, and then call to get the different rates. In the one-way rental market rates can vary dramatically and many of the best rates are from the largest car rental companies rather than the smaller operators who might have normally lower daily return-to-the-same-location rates.

For example: We called each of the major automobile rental companies as well as some of the smaller operators. The rental rates for the same market varied in one case from $227 to $446 for the same three-day one-way rental. Another scenario resulted in a low cost of $195 versus a high of $519 for a weekly one-way rental.

AAA's deal with Hertz

The American Automobile Association (AAA) has an arrangement with Hertz that becomes one of the best discounts available. AAA members are guaranteed the lowest available rates, discounts up to 20 percent and promotional coupon programs. Hertz also waives any normal Saturday night stayover requirement as well as additional driver charges for AAA members. They also provide improved insurance benefits with a $3,000 liability cap and limited primary personal liability insurance.

At press time no other automobile rental companies have similar contracts with AAA but virtually all rental car companies offer AAA discounts.

Local taxes, fees and surcharges

These added costs can add more than 23 percent to a quoted rental charge. Car rental companies are not required to include them in advertisements since they are not assessed for every rental.

There is not much travelers can do about these taxes and fees, but knowing how much you will be dunned when you return the car eliminates the surprise and eases the impact.

For the most part the taxes are simply an extension of a state and city's normal sales tax. Other states and cities add special taxes to every car rental. Still other states, cities, airports and municipalities add additional fees and surcharges to your rental car bill.

These fees and surcharges are assessed for everything from easing Boston's burden of uncollected parking tickets and paying for auto licenses in California, to rebuilding highways and disposing of old batteries, oil and tires. Other fees, depending on the airport, are charged for picking up passengers at the terminal, building new baseball and football stadiums, and expanding convention facilities.

Ask the rental agent when you pick up your car about the additional fees and taxes. That way, you'll have an idea of what the charge will be when you return the car. Don't expect the rental car reservation agent to have a clue about the local taxes and fees, though you may be lucky enough to get a list when you make your reservation.

Screening driver's licenses

A new twist to automobile rentals is a growing system of screening driving records. Big Brother has definitely arrived at many rental car companies. Now many car rental companies screen the Department of Motor Vehicles (DMV) records of drivers requesting a rental car in a growing number of states. Yes, the rental company computer accesses your home state driving record from the DMV computers.

Everyone gets checked. All state DMVs are required to share driving records with rental car companies. The biggest differences in these driver record checks comes when one state is computerized and another is not. Clearly, drivers from states with computerized DMVs will have much more accessible driver records.

✔ If you have had an accident within the last two or three years the companies may refuse to rent you a car based on their criteria—basically, if there was any personal injury or a fatality you may be out of luck. Other no-nos include driving intoxicated, leaving the scene of an accident and suspended or revoked licenses. Most rental firms are creating a blacklist, so if you are refused rental in one state, you will probably be refused rental everywhere.

If you are with a client on a business trip, this may be downright embarrassing.

✔ NOTE: Driver's licenses are checked when you show up to rent the car rather than at the time of the reservation. This makes getting another car from another company, especially another car at a similar rate, difficult, if indeed possible.

❑ When you are refused a rental you have no tested rights—even if the DMV records are in error.

❏ Check your driving record at your state DMV.

❏ Ask before you arrive at the rental counter whether the auto rental company screens driver's licenses.

❏ If you have been found unfit for a rental because of a license check you will have to find a company that does not check licenses. Call your DMV and find out what you can do to clear your record. But be aware, in some states there is no erasing any accident record.

❏ To check your driving record contact your DMV or call TML Information Services at 1-800-388-9099. They perform about 80 percent of the checks for car rental companies. They will perform a personal check of your record for $9.95 (or $7.95 for AAA members). It only takes a few minutes and a credit card for payment.

In the rental companies' defense, these checks were prompted by liability laws in New York, Florida and about 10 other states which have vicarious liability laws that hold the automobile owner responsible for the damages caused by it, even when operated by someone else. Unfortunately, what began as a defense against massive personal-injury awards in a few states has spread to affect all of us.

Check your rental car
Basics to look for

What happens if you have a flat tire and the spare is also flat, or the lug wrench is missing? Or what can the rental car company do for you when you reach the top of a mountain pass and find that the snow chains provided are the wrong size—worse yet, too small? What if you discover, after lunch, a crumpled fender you didn't notice before you left the lot?

In these cases you are normally up the proverbial creek without a paddle. So protect yourself and check out any car you are getting ready to rent.

❑   If there is anything else amiss, have it repaired or noted on the rental agreement before you leave the lot. Make sure it is documented.

❑   Check the spare and make sure you have the basic automobile tool kit with the lug wrench and jack.

❑   If you are picking up chains, carefully ensure that they are the proper ones for your tires.

❑   Do a walk-around and check for broken lights, scratches and dents, or other damage you may be held responsible for.

❑   Note which side the fuel filler door is on. This is only a little thing, but can ease hassles at your first filling station.

❑   If you are paying for mileage, make sure to check the odometer and note the level of the gas tank. If mileage doesn't match the rental form, or if the tank isn't full, let the attendant know.

Rental car breakdowns

What happens if your rental car transmission freezes in reverse, or you lose power and find yourself stranded on the highway, or the engine just won't start?

This is where bigger is better. The larger rental agencies such as Hertz, Avis, Budget or National can provide a real advantage over the smaller ones. Since the large companies have more rental locations, it is easier to get another car and to get help. Other large agencies like Alamo or Dollar can also provide good assistance, depending on how close you are to one of their offices. Smaller agencies with fewer locations just can't help as quickly and conveniently.

▲ **Alamo** roadside service is 800-803-4444.

▲ **Avis** has a nationwide toll-free hotline (800-345-2847) that will send any distress call automatically to the nearest Avis outlet providing road service. Some of their phone systems let you know the closest 24-hour location.

▲ **Budget** has phone numbers in the rental contract; you can also call the 24-hour reservations number with your problem (800-527-0700).

▲ **Dollar** has a similar arrangement with the Cross Country Motor Club. Their number is 800-235-9393.

▲ **Hertz** provides a toll-free number (800-654-5060) and claims to be able to have renters back on the road in less than an hour in most cases. Alternatively, they send renters to appointments by taxi or other transport.

▲ **National** has an agreement with the Cross Country Motor Club, which has 15,000 service and towing affiliates and 24-hour service. Call 800-367-6767. They also handle flats and low batteries.

International car-rental considerations

Driving or renting cars outside of the United States means dealing with an entirely different set of rules and laws. The law changes whether you pick up your car abroad or drive from the U.S. to Canada or Mexico.

International rentals

When a U.S. citizen or resident is planning to rent an automobile in Europe or elsewhere outside of the country, it is important that the reservation be made here in the United States for pickup in Europe or elsewhere. The savings are significant and are sometimes even more than 50 percent.

A good place to start checking on automobile rental rates is with Auto Europe (1-800-223-5555), a rental car consolidator, that guarantees the lowest prices for rentals picked up in Europe. They also will provide a US$ rate which will be guaranteed in dollars (for Canada the guarantee is in Canadian dollars), so tourists do not have to worry about changes in exchange rates.

Check on the minimum driving ages in Europe. Most rental agencies require that drivers be 25 years of age or traveling on business to rent a car.

International one-way rentals

When renting automobiles in Europe the drop-off rules change. This is the basic drop-off rule in Europe—pick up and drop off in the same country means you pay no drop-off charge.

There are variations on the theme that all work to the rental car clients' advantage. One such rule is that with some international rentals of 21 days or longer, renters may pick up a car in Switzerland and drop it off in France, Germany, Italy or the Netherlands with no drop-off charge.

> **NOTE:** These rules vary from company to company and they are in effect only for relatively long-term rentals.

Hertz has a program called Rent it Here/Leave it There that allows travelers in Europe to pick up a car in one country and drop it off in another with a drop-off fee of only about US$100–125. This program links more than 100 cities and 200 Hertz locations in eight countries. Call Hertz for details. The countries are France, Germany, Italy, Belgium, Luxembourg, Switzerland, Austria and the Netherlands. Call for specifics. There are quirks such as Dutch cars are not allowed to be dropped off in Italy.

A unique one-way convenience is Le Swap where Hertz in conjunction with the Channel Tunnel allows travelers to swap their right-hand-drive rental car in Calais for a left-hand-drive car (or vice-versa). This program works between the U.K. and rental locations in Germany, Belgium, France, Luxembourg and the Netherlands.

International credit-card collision damage insurance

❏ If you use credit card CDW overseas, it is automatically considered primary coverage.

❏ Special conditions exist in some countries, specifically New Zealand and Australia, which require you to purchase local insurance regardless of credit card coverage. An "approval" will also be placed on your credit card for gas (about $40) and the insurance deductible (around $500 in most cases).

❏ Some foreign automobile rental agencies (and a few in the U.S.) may place a hold on a certain amount of your card credit. In some cases this may push the card over your credit limit.

✔ NOTE: One solution to credit-card holds is to travel with two credit cards.

❑ Credit holds are most common in the Caribbean and South America. Make sure to ask the car-rental reservationist whether a hold or deposit will be required. But beware: even if you get everything in writing here in the U.S., it may be worthless overseas. So plan on having to leave a deposit.

❑ Credit card CDW in most cases is limited to either two weeks or one month. If you are planning a longer rental you can turn in your car at the end of the credit card insurance period and rent it again. If you do this it would be best to use a different credit card for the second rental. This works and is legal, but it is often difficult depending on your travels. Another option is to look into a purchase lease of a car in a foreign country. These purchase lease arrangements often provide insurance as part of the lease price and they are normally less expensive than a straight rental.

❑ If you are not using a credit card be aware that almost all U.S. automobile insurance policies are not in effect when driving outside the U.S. or Canada. Personal car insurance rarely provides foreign coverage, owing to the variety of international insurance regulations and standards.

❑ American Express Cards do not insure cars rented in Jamaica, Ireland, Israel, Italy, Australia and New Zealand.

International Driver's Permit

Though Canada and most countries in Europe recognize a U.S. driver's license, several such as Italy, Austria and Germany require local translations of the documents. For all other countries your best bet is to get an International Driving Permit from AAA.

International Driving Permits are good for a year. Start the process by mail a month before your departure. If you live near an AAA office, you can accomplish the entire process, including photos, in less than a hour. International Driving Permits cost $10. Call (800) AAA-HELP for the forms and the location of the nearest office issuing permits. In Canada call (800) 336-HELP. You'll need:

❏ your license

❏ two passport-type photos, color or black and white (those from a dime-store photo booth are fine). If you have photos taken at a AAA office the cost is $8 for members, $10 for nonmembers.

Rules for driving to Canada and Mexico

Driving a rental car or your own car to Mexico or Canada requires a bit of preparation, especially if you are heading down Mexico way.

Canada:

❏ You need a U.S. driver's license, and remember to carry your passport or birth certificate to get back to the U.S.

❏ You must have minimum liability insurance equivalent to Cdn$200,000 (about US$160,000) everywhere except in the province of Quebec where the minimum is Cdn$50,000 (about US$40,000).

❏ Most U.S. insurers cover drivers in Canada, but you should make sure. Though insurance cards are rarely asked for, have your insurance company send you a **Canadian Non-Resident Inter-Provincial Motor Vehicle Liability Insurance Card.**

Credit card CDW works in Canada, but you'll need your own insurance to provide liability coverage.

Mexico:

❏ **Get ready for red tape.** You will need a passport or certified copy of your birth certificate, valid U.S. driver's license, and Mexican Tourist Card (no-cost from Mexican consulates or at the border) if you plan to stay more than three days.

❏ If you are taking your own car further than the immediate border area (loosely defined as within 10 to 12 miles of any border crossing) you'll need to take the original of your title or registration plus a copy. Then when you hit the border station for cars, about 12 miles inside the Mexican border, you can get your driving permit by paying $10 with a credit card issued by a bank outside Mexico. If you are driving a company car or a friend's car bring along a notarized letter authorizing you to drive the car, signed by the proper owner or the owner's representative.

❏ A border state AAA program issues all immigration and customs forms. Fees vary.

❏ Your stateside insurance is probably no good in Mexico. You'll have to buy Mexican liability insurance from an office at the border crossing, from AAA or from the rental agency if you take a rental car. Credit-card collision waiver is good in Mexico.

❏ This routine is the same with rental car or personal auto. If you rent in Mexico you pay a very stiff price but eliminate much of the hassle.

NOTE: Most rental agencies in San Diego, California and San Antonio, Texas, as well as most major agencies near the Mexican border do not allow you to take their rental cars into Mexico.

Swiss and Austrian highway taxes

Tolls on superhighways in Switzerland are assessed as an annual road tax. If you don't want to drive on a superhighway, you don't pay the tax. However, for most of us traveling through Switzerland on vacation or business the superhighways are vital to move through the country quickly.

When the calendar-year toll is paid, a Swiss Autobahn decal is attached to the window of the car. Most rental cars in Europe have this toll paid. But if you are picking up a car at one end of Europe and driving through Switzerland, check to see whether the highway toll decal is in the window. If you arrive in Switzerland without the decal you will have to pay about $25 for one. Most rental companies will reimburse you for the cost, but if you don't know about this rule it can be a pain.

Austria also has a superhighway tax. Rather than issuing stickers that show cars have paid the tax for a year, the Austrian system charges for shorter periods of time. Upon entering Austria, drivers planning to use the Autobahn system must pay a highway tax based on the length of time they are planning to stay in the country. A ten-day highway sticker costs about US$6. This highway tax is your responsibility. It will not be reimbursed by the rental car company.

Renting cars in Eastern Europe

If you are planning a trip to Eastern Europe—Poland, the Czech Republic, the Slovak Republic, Hungary, Bulgaria or Romania—you may have to finesse your automobile rental because of the high rates of theft and vandalism.

Check with your rental agency or travel agency for the current rules and regulations when you make your arrangements.

Hertz, for example, has a labyrinthine group of rules without seeming rhyme or reason. Here are some sample rules related to me by Hertz—cars rented in Austria may be taken to the Czech Republic, Slovakia and Hungary, but no other eastern-European countries; rentals from Denmark, Finland and Spain can be taken to the Czech Republic, Bulgaria, Hungary, Poland, Romania and Slovakia; automobiles rented from Norway may be taken into Romania and Hungary; and finally all these rentals require the cars to be dropped off in the country of rental.

Hertz is not alone, all other car rental companies have restrictions that vary from company to company and from country to country. For example:

❏ One company allows only cars rented in Switzerland to be taken into Eastern Europe.

❏ One limits East-West travel with rental cars to Austria and Hungary; another limits rentals to trips between Austria, Hungary and the Czech Republic.

❏ Many companies require you to purchase their own CDW.

❏ Several large European rental agencies won't allow any cars to cross into Eastern Europe.

❏ The French and Belgians offer automobile *leases*, which have no restrictions.

According to the credit card companies, their collision damage waiver is good throughout Eastern Europe, but finding a rental company who will accept the insurance can be difficult.

✔ **NOTE:** Unleaded gas is next to impossible to find. If you are planning a trip into Eastern Europe, rent a car that takes normal leaded gas. Eastern Germany has plenty of unleaded gas pumps and Hungary has a respectable number, but they are hard to find.

🚗RENTAL FACT🚗

✔ China, Egypt and Nepal do not permit foreigners to drive, and all rental cars come with chauffeurs.

Internet Sites for Travelers

Airlines on the Internet

Airlines, from the largest to the smallest, have developed an Internet presence. Some allow travelers to make reservations and pay for flights. Some airlines' sites provide special "online airfares" available for weekend travel and other last-minute deals. Some provide detailed information on travel for unaccompanied children, seniors and pets. This is an area of travel in a major state of development. Over the next years anyone trying to get Travel Rights information may have a new place to look for hard-to-get rules.

Interestingly, none of the major, international airline sites provide passengers with a Contract of Carriage, the contract travelers "sign" whenever they purchase an airline ticket. Though federal regulations require that the airlines make the Contract of Carriage available at all ticket offices and at airports served by each airline, most airlines have decided to leave the Contract of Carriage out of their Web sites. We found a complete Contract of Carriage on only the Southwest Airlines and Reno Air sites. The United Airlines' Contract of Carriage can be found on the Internet but it is not easy to find. It can be found online at http://www.sirius.com/~eps/UA/UA/dgr-1/Welcome.html.

Several Internet sites have been developed by the computer reservation systems (CRS) that allow a user to search for flights and fares from many different airlines. Some of these sites provide a lowest-cost search which never seems to work perfectly, but provides some direction for those looking for the best airfare in various markets.

The Internet and all travel-related Web sites are a work in progress. These Web sites were reviewed in early 1998. Though the specifics of the sites may change, the list of URLs (Uniform Resource Locators) will remain useful for anyone searching for Internet information.

Perhaps the most important part of these pages is the list of URLs or the Internet address of the airlines. The actual airline Web sites are undergoing constant change and improvements.

General travel reservation system Web sites

Easy Sabre (http://www.easysabre.com). This is the granddaddy of online reservation systems. Users can check fares and reservations for virtually every airline in the world and make reservations. This system holds your seat preferences, special meal requirements and frequent flyer numbers.

Worldspan (http://www.worldspan.com) is another large international CRS owned mostly by Delta, Northwest, TWA. This site does not offer reservations as of press time, but has many links to other sites where the reservation system is operational.

Microsoft Expedia (http://expedia.msn.com) is one of the most active sites in terms of deals and specials. This site is exceptional in its coverage of discounted airfares such as senior and child fares. It offers an electronic newsletter that alerts travelers to good deals. Once you register (only takes a few minutes) check fares and make reservations on the Website. Expedia also has easy-to-use hotel and car rental information. There are many other features such as driving directions, a travel magazine, maps, special vacation deals, and so on.

Travelocity (http://www.travelocity.com) works together with American Airlines' sister CRS, Sabre. Make reservations and pay for airlines, hotels and automobiles. The site has loads of destination information. Though travelers will be prompted for a credit card number to access the system, they can hold reservations without buying them.

FLIFO (http://www.flifo.com) farebuster feature is good (finds cheaper alternative flights) but you have to go through the booking process to find out if they are available.

1travel.com (http://www.1travel.com) is a bargain hunters heaven. This site links with consolidators of airline tickets, hotels and automobile rentals. Check out the excellent travel rules section including airline rules for many travel problems. A lowest-fare search system, called TravelWiz™, works best when using a toll-free number 1-800-929-2523, but can also be accessed online. They promise an online response within 24 hours. This site is massive with an excellent interface and takes hours to exhaust.

Internet Travel Network (http://www.itn.net) is a great travel site with a good reservation engine. This site has reservations for air, car, hotels, vacation packages and is growing. The flight reservation/information is very quick and easy to use.

Preview Travel (http://www.reservations.com) similar to Expedia and ITN, but same specifications did not bring up similar flights—the lowest fares available do not coincide with what the other websites say. It has fairly quick good tips on finding low fares (under "Farefinder").

Trax Software (http://www.trax.com) is similar to FLIFO, ITN and Travelweb. You have to select your flights before the prices are shown, but then they have the cheaper alternative option available. It's not as glitzy as Travelocity or ITN, but works pretty well.

System One (http://www.sys1.com/), less gimmicky than all the others—you type in your route and dates and it gives you a listing of flights and the lowest possible fares. Seems more comprehensive than the others. However...you can't purchase tickets online. Instead, contact one of the agencies they use (they give you a list, based on your location). A very convenient site for people who want to do it this way.

TripWeb (http://www.tripweb.com) uses System One, but you can make reservations directly from the fare-finder. It has nice additional features such as free flight insurance. The system guarantees finding lowest fares (or double the difference back) but it will not make reservations on flights within 7 days.

Travelweb (http://www.travelweb.com) has a lot of travel information and graphics. It uses ITN and suggests cheaper alternative flights.

TISS (http://www.tiss.com) is an online database provided by a group of consolidators and from Travelocity departing from several Asian and European airports (they plan to add other countries). They claim the prices they offer are the best available.

Destinations Unlimited (http://www.air-fare.com) lists lowest fares among 40 major U.S. cities, with daily updates, reservations and ticketing.

BizTravel.com (http://www.biztravel.com/V4/ newhome.cfm) is designed for business travelers. It offers flight reservations, a frequent flyer mileage tracking program, flight operations, and other business traveler information on destinations and more.

Yahoo! Travel
(http://travel.yahoo.com/destinations/) This site offers reservation capabilities for air, auto and lodging. This site is powered by Travelocity.

Airline Web Sites

Many airlines are on the World Wide Web. For most of them you need a browser that supports forms, such as Netscape, or Internet Explorer. Several good directories of airlines are:

http://www.yahoo.com/Business/Corporations/ Travel/Airlines

http://www.itn.net/airlines

http://pages.prodigy.com/airport/air2.htm

http://shoga.wwa.com/~dcorsi/airline.html

http://www.ita-travel.com/air.html.

There are plenty more and these sites seem to be growing, but this list will get anyone started.

Individual airline sites

The airlines listed here all have schedule or booking information available; see the pages mentioned above for many more airline Web pages with other information. The best way to navigate through most of these airline Web sites is to call up the site index or use the search function. I have found that this provides the easiest way to find all the information on the site such as baggage rules, unaccompanied minors, Contract of Carriage, and so on.

In the discussions below, flight operations means online notice of delays, gates, cancellations, and the like. Ticketless ticketing means the airline sends you a receipt with a record locater number. You use that number and show ID when you check in (your name, ID and flight number normally works fine). They send the receipt via e-mail, fax, or (if there's time) snail mail. You pay for your tickets online or through an 800 number with a credit card.

Air Canada (http://www.aircanada.ca:80/ac_world/schedule/) has schedule information and weekly Websaver special fares (also in French).

Alaska Airlines (http://www.alaska-air.com/) has a Web site with flight information, reservations, and ticketless ticketing.

American Airlines (http://www.americanair.com/) has schedules, fares, and flight operations. Reservations and ticketing are through AAccess with an AAdvantage number.

America West (http://www.americawest.com) has schedule information, reservations, and electronic ticketing in an attractive site. Includes information on minors, seniors, baggage and pets.

American Trans Air (http://www.ata.com) site has schedules, fares, flight operations and reservations.

Austrian Airlines (http://www.Austria.EU.net:81/aua/) offers a fairly useless site that is confusing and seems to be devoid of consumer information.

British Airways (http://www.british-airways.com/) has so-so schedule information, no connections. Slim pickings.

British Midland (http://www.iflybritishmidland.com/) has a Web-based booking and ticketing system called CyberSeat, which lets you reserve and buy tickets and little else.

Canadian Airlines (http://www.cdnair.ca) has schedule information, Web special fares, and downloadable dial-up schedule and reservations software, but no reservations via the Web site.

Continental (http://www.flycontinental.com) has schedules and booking. CO.O.L. system offers a general purpose reservation system with hotels and cars as well as flights. Lots of consumer information.

Delta (http://www.delta-air.com) has schedules, reservations and flight operations. The site also has some other consumer information—baggage rules, movie schedules, meal choices, airport maps, etc.

El Al (http://www.elal.co.il) has U.S. schedules and some U.S.-oriented package information.

Finnair (http://www.us.finnair.com/) has limited schedule information.

KLM Royal Dutch Airline (http://www.klm.nl/) has flight operations, very limited schedules and availability but no reservations capability, consumer information such as baggage rules, unaccompanied minor rules and special meals. Schedule does not specify whether flight is on KLM or NW aircraft. Links to Northwest site with online booking.

Lufthansa Info Flyway (http://www.lufthansa.com) offers schedules (for most airlines, not just Lufthansa) and booking. Otherwise not too much for the consumer.

LTU Airline (http://www.ltu.com/ltu) offers low-fares to Germany and good tourist information.

Northwest Airlines (http://www.nwa.com/home.html) has online booking, schedule and fare information, flights operations, "Cyber Savers," and vacation packages.

Pan American (http://www.flypanam.com) has the basics with cyberfares as well, but no reservations.

Qantas (http://www.qantas.com) has a site with schedules and flight operations.

Reno Air (http://www.renoair.com/) has schedules and ticketless reservations on their excellent and informative site. This site includes Contract of Carriage and loads of information to help any passenger.

Sabena (http://www.sabena.com/) has minimal trans-Atlantic schedule information.

SAS (http://www.flysas.com/) has schedule information online, great links to other related sites and also has a downloadable worldwide schedule.

Singapore Airlines (http://www.singaporeair.com) has schedules and other information such as lost ticket rules, infant rules, corporate information.

South African Airways (http://www.saa.co.za/saa/frameset_main_contents.html) has a busy site with schedules and a little destination information.

Southwest Airlines (http://www.iflyswa.com) has schedules and fares, and now reservations and ticketless ticketing. One of the best airline sites complete with Contract of Carriage.

Swissair (http://www.swissair.ch) has schedules and provides online booking. The site index provides the best method of negotiating the site.

TWA (http://www.twa.com) has schedules, reservations, weekly Web specials and a wide range of information.

United (http://www.ual.com) has a site divided between airline and traveler. The airline site does not have the Contract of Carriage. I never got the reservation system to work, but it seems to be part of the

ITN system noted above. United has an Internet fare program called E-Savers.

USAirways (http://www.usair.com/) has schedules and airline information, but no reservations.

Varig (http://www.varig.com.br) has schedule information. It is in Portuguese, Spanish or English.

Internet bargain airfares

Airlines occasionally offer special fares or promotions to Internet users.

Air Canada (http://www.aircanada.ca:80/ac_world/schedule/) has weekly Websaver special fares.

American Airlines has a mailing list for "Net SAAver fares," otherwise unadvertised specials from Chicago or Dallas. Sign up and make reservations on their Web page **(http://www.americanair.com/aa_home/aans.html)**.

American Trans Air (http://www.ata.com) has "net fares," special fares available only on their Web site.

Canadian Airlines (http://www.cdnair.ca) has weekly Web fares, posted every Wednesday. Reservations are supported in French and English.

Cathay Pacific Airlines (http://www.cathay-usa.com) has a contest (first prize: a fancy trip from the U.S. to Hong Kong), seat auctions, and other inducements to buy. You have to register in their free "Cybertraveller" at the Web site.

Continental (http://www.flycontinental.com/q3/cooltravel/cooltravel.html) has a mailing list for net-only specials.

Finnair (http://www.us.finnair.com/) has occasional seat auctions.

Northwest (http://www.nwa.com/travel/nwapr/ index.shtml) has promotions including a few Cyber-Saver fares.

South African Airways (http://www.saa.co.za/saa) provides auctioned airfares on a regular basis.

TWA (http://www.twa.com) has weekly Web specials.

United (http://www.ual.com) offers E-Savers that can be accessed through the Internet Travel Network as well.

USAirways (http://www.usair.com/travel/fares/ esavers.html) has an "e-savers" mailing list with weekly special fares from Boston, Pittsburgh and Philadelphia, other cities to be added.

Automobile Rental Companies on the Web

For a complete list of automobile rental company sites call up **(http://www.yahoo.com/Business_and_ Economy/Companies/Automotive/Rentals/)**

AutoEurope (http://www.auto-europe.com/) is one of the most consumer-friendly sites on the Net. This site includes not only automobile rentals, but also airline and hotel reservations. The list of travel links under "reference" is one of the best on the Net.

Alamo Automobile Rental (http://www.goalamo.com/)

Avis Car Rental (http://www.avis.com/)

Budget Rent a Car (http://www.budgetrentacar.com/)

Dollar Rent a Car (http://www.dollarcar.com/)

Hertz (http://www.hertz.com/)

Kemwel (http://www.kemwel.com/) has good deals for rentals in Europe.

National Car Rental (http://www.nationalcar.com/)

Thrifty (http://www.thrifty.com/)

These sites all provide online reservations, fleet descriptions and locations. The basics.

BreezeNet's Guide to Airport Rental Cars (http://www.bnm.com/rcar.htm#top) is a one-stop car rental site for quick direct online reservations to auto rental companies with airport service. Includes coupons, discounts, rates, phone numbers and tips for rental cars at major U.S. & international airports. For car rentals in Canada check out **http://www.bnm.com/can.htm.**

Other general travel sites:

Amtrak (http://www.amtrak.com) offers a rail travel site for parts of the U.S. Schedule information and reservations are available.

Via Rail Canada (http://www.viarail.ca) provides rail information and is most competitive in the Montreal-Ottawa-Toronto corridor. Includes schedule and fare information, but has no reservations capability (also available in French).

TheTrip (http://www.thetrip.com/) is a general travel site with excellent commentary as well as reservation systems for airlines, car rentals, and hotels plus reviews of restaurants, currency conversion and lodging discounts all with maps.

Xplore Travel (http://www.xplore.com/xplore500/medium/travel.html) provides links to top travel sites on the Web. When we went into the site there were links with: American Express Travel,

Biztravel.com, City.Net, Destinations Magazine, Epicurious Travel, Fodor's Travel Online, Frommer's Encyclopedia of Travel, Go West, Great Outdoor Recreation Pages, Internet Travel Network, Lonely Planet, MapQuest!, Microsoft Expedia, National Park Service, Preview Travel, Roadside America, Rough Guides, TheTrip.com, Travel Channel Online Network, Travel Health Online, Traveler.Net, Travelocity, TravelWeb, World Travel Guide.

Air Travel Pro (http://www.dfw.net/~morris/index. html) is another collection of links organized into a table format. Links are more far reaching than those on Xplore. These include: airlines, hotels, maps, B&Bs, car rentals, taxi fares and more.

Travel Links (http://www.travellinks.com/lookup. html) provides links to air, lodging, cruises, rail, tour operators, travel agents, casinos and convention and visitor's bureaus.

Travel Health Information (http://www.travelhealth .com) is everything that the name implies, and then some, with consulate, embassy and passport links.

TravelFile (http://www.travelfile.com/) is a series of searchable directories containing over 100,000 files of information on travel suppliers, tourism offices, attractions, and events for destinations worldwide.

City.Net (http://www.city.net/) a very comprehensive international guide to communities around the world. City.Net provides easy and timely access to information on travel, entertainment, and local business, plus government and community services for all regions of the world.

Traveler.Net (http://www.traveler.net/) one of the Web's leading index of travel resources—thousands of links, news and travel tips and special values on hotels and resorts around the world.

NoJetLag (http://www.nojetlag.com) has lots of jet lag information as well as a series of wonderful links to other travel Web sites.

This travel site **(http://www.sites.com/travel/)** is loaded with travel links, links and more links.

Medical alerts are listed on this university site **(http://weber.u. washington.edu/%7Etravmed)**. This site is also linked with other major health sites.

On The Road (http://www.roadnews.com) is a treasure trove of information for those traveling with a laptop computer anywhere in the world. It includes signup for a newsletter packed with techniques to get up and running internationally with a laptop. This is also one of the best link sites for air reservations, discount tickets, and airport Web sites.

Best Fares (http://www.bestfares.com) is the jackpot for fare bargains. The free part of the site has net specials, bargains that only last a few hours, a travel scam alert, airline links, airports, airport codes, special meals, airline movie schedules, rail links, weather and more. The subscriber section has in-depth travel bargains and coupon deal coverage.

Department of Transportation (http://www.dot.gov) has a site packed with information including airline consumer publications, Fly Rights, and airline reports such as on-time reports, lost luggage and overbooking statistics. Look under Office of the Secretary then Office of General Counsel.

Tax-free Shopping (http://www.taxfree.se/index0.html) provides the basics for getting VAT refunds.

WebFlyer (http://www.insideflyer.com) is packed with frequent flyer information.

Travel Facts (http://www.travelfacts.com) is brilliant with deals, schedules, links, and some destinations.

Rand McNally (http://www.randmcnally.com) is full of travel gems like a links to state transportation departments and festivals and events in a searchable database. Site links with ITN for reservations.

ABC News (http://www.abcnews.com/sections/travel/) has good timely travel information and columns with an attitude like The Crabby Traveler.

NBC/MSNBC (http://www.nbcnews.com/news/LIV_Front.asp) has a series of travel articles in the living section of their site.

CNN (http://www.cnn.com/TRAVEL/) has a little bit of everything, all well done, from currency to destinations and online reservations for about everything.

Travel magazines online

Condé Nast Traveler (http://travel.epicurious.com/travel/g_cnt/00_home_page/home.html) has features plus the helpful Ombudsman section for help with travel problems. Click on consumer help.

Outside Online (http://outside.starwave.com/index.html) and **Outside Magazine (http://outside.starwave.com:80/magazine/omindex.html)** provide an excellent site duo for adventure travel.

Travel and Leisure (http://www.travelandleisure.com) has good destination pieces and excellent links to tourist boards and travel providers. Click "more features" then "departments" for travel tips.

National Geographic Traveler (http://www.nationalgeographic.com/media/traveler/) is a wonderful site with lush destination articles and illustrations. Look under Internet resources for phenomenal consumer links to newspapers, currency rates, travel information, embassies and more.

CREDIT CARD

BENEFITS

Travelers should take a careful look at the benefits of their credit cards. MasterCard, Visa and Discover are credit and charge cards that allow payments for travel and purchases over a period of time. American Express and Diners Club are travel and entertainment cards that require full payment of the balance each month (except in the case of airline tickets, which may be paid for over several months with American Express).

Credit cards can be used either to obtain credit and stretch the payment period or as a travel tool to allow additional flexibility and consumer protection. In the first case, just looking for the card with the lowest interest rate and annual fee is the governing factor. However, when looking at a credit card as a travel tool, everything requires a different focus. This chapter outlines the benefits different credit and charge cards offer travelers. There is no way to cover *all* the fine print here. We only can provide a look at the most important considerations.

As noted in the Auto Rights chapter, many corporate and individual credit cards provide collision damage insurance. American Express, Diners Club, Discover, Visa and MasterCard also provide an array of wide-ranging and quite valuable insurance coverages. Not much has been made of this by the travel media. Conventional wisdom is that these coverages merely duplicate what you already have. But such wisdom can be very short-sighted when some of the benefits of gold cards and business cards are taken into account.

Additional coverages provided by various cards are impressive, and all are in effect worldwide unless specifically limited. The basic benefits that are most important to travelers are shown below. These coverages vary card by card and bank by bank—read your cardmember agreement carefully.

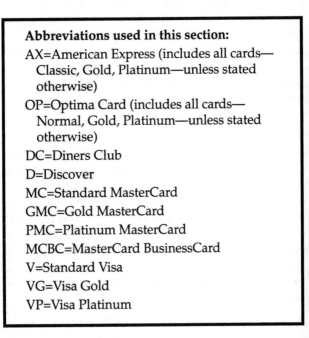

Abbreviations used in this section:

AX=American Express (includes all cards—Classic, Gold, Platinum—unless stated otherwise)

OP=Optima Card (includes all cards—Normal, Gold, Platinum—unless stated otherwise)

DC=Diners Club

D=Discover

MC=Standard MasterCard

GMC=Gold MasterCard

PMC=Platinum MasterCard

MCBC=MasterCard BusinessCard

V=Standard Visa

VG=Visa Gold

VP=Visa Platinum

Life and property insurance

● Buyer protection benefit or Purchase Assurance
(MC, GMC, AX, D)

Once upon a time, this was offered by virtually every card to U.S. (the 50 states, D.C., Puerto Rico, and U.S. Virgin Islands) cardholders. Visa has curtailed the protection (different banks issuing Visa cards include the coverage, others don't), but MasterCard still offers it with most cards. American Express was the leader in creating this benefit and still offers it with all its cards. It protects any purchases made with your card against damage and theft for (normally) 90 days from date of purchase. This protection is limited to $1,000 per occurrence for most cards with a variable monetary limit per card (normally about $50,000).

This is often secondary insurance which pays after you have already been indemnified by your homeowner, auto or renter's insurance. It is excellent for covering deductibles.

✔ TRAVELER'S NOTE: Items stolen from a car, whether left in the car or part of the automobile equipment, are not covered. Items stolen or damaged in checked baggage are not covered. Hand baggage is covered. Gifts purchased with the card that you give to others are also covered. Confiscation by customs officials is not covered nor are Acts of God, war or hostilities of any kind.

IMPORTANT NOTE: Stolen items *must* be reported to the police or an appropriate authority within 36 to 45 hours. Failure to get a police report will negate any coverage.

● **Automatic travel accident insurance**
(V, VG, MC, GMC, MCBC, AX, DC, D)

This insurance comes into effect when travel on common carriers is purchased with a credit card. Diners Club also provides this benefit when traveling on free tickets such as frequent flyer tickets.

The coverage is relatively gruesome, dealing with death and dismemberment. The only point here is to be aware that you (or another who may have charged tickets) may have additional insurance for injury or death while traveling on any public carrier be it train, plane, ship, airport shuttle, or other transport from the time of leaving home for the airport or terminal until returning home. Coverage depends on the type of card you have.

Some examples:
American Express Classic, Gold, and Corporate Card coverage is $100,000; American Express Platinum coverage is $500,000.

Coverage is negotiated by the issuing bank for Visa and MasterCards—the First Card Visa Gold and Capitol One Gold MasterCard provide $250,000; most classic Visa and MasterCard cards provide $100,000. Check for your specific coverage.

Discover offers $500,000 of insurance.

☆ Diners Club provides the best coverage with this type of insurance. It not only provides $350,000 of life insurance if travelers purchase their tickets with their Diners Club credit card, but also offers coverage for current Diners Club members traveling on free tickets such as frequent flyer awards.

NOTE: Make sure heirs are aware of this additional insurance coverage. It can be a significant part of an estate.

Travel assistance services

You can call a toll-free number provided by your credit card and receive information that will help you plan your trip and help if things go wrong *during* your trip. These benefits can be real time-savers, and the money transfer features save you money. Perhaps the best part of these services is that the card travel service center can serve almost as a secretary and message center in an emergency. This includes:

✦ Information on passport and visa requirements, immunizations, currency exchange rates and weather forecasts.

✦ Arranging to transfer up to $5,000 from a family member, friend or business.

✦ Assisting in replacement of important documents including lost passports and tickets. You are responsible for the cost of replacements.

✦ Help in locating luggage if it is lost by a common carrier. Transport of luggage to your location is at your expense.

✔ **NOTE:** If you have a Gold MasterCard, Visa Gold, American Express, Diners Club, or MasterCard BusinessCard and you travel more than 50 or 100 miles away from your home (depending on the card) additional travel assistance programs take effect generally as follows (specifics vary depending on the card):

● **Worldwide legal referral assistance**

   (VG, GMC, MCBC, AX, DC)

   Referrals to English-speaking attorneys and contact with U.S. embassies and consulates will be arranged in case of arrest, an automobile accident or need of other legal assistance. In addition most credit card companies can assist in transferring bail payments from your personal accounts or your credit card credit line. The assistance centers normally follow up to ensure that the bail is handled properly.

● **Emergency message services**

(VG, GMC, MCBC, AX, DC)

Credit card assistance centers will pass along emergency messages to friends, family and business associates. This allows you to make only one call to the assistance center. They do the rest. I've know folks who used this service to tell relatives planning to meet them at the airport that they were stuck in a major weather delay.

● **Emergency transportation and medical assistance**

(VG, GMC, MCBC, AX, DC)

If you become ill or are injured during a trip, most credit card assistance centers will help make arrangements to bring you home or transfer you to another hospital. These assistance centers will all arrange to get children home and provide continuing contact with family members. In the event of death, these travel assistance programs help with the transfer of remains back home. They will also assist in making travel arrangements to bring a family member or close friend to your bedside if you are traveling alone and have a travel emergency. All expenses are paid for by the cardmember or the cardmember's estate.

Both Visa and MasterCard Gold cards will assist in filling prescriptions. If the prescriptions are not locally available, they will arrange for delivery.

☆ MasterCardBusinessCard goes several big steps further than just assistance with their unique MasterAssist/Medical program. These benefits are available to card holders regardless of what method was used to pay for the trip. *(These specific benefits only apply to MasterCard BusinessCards, not any other type of MasterCard.)*

• This credit card will actually pay for any transfers necessary due to an accident or sudden illness while traveling more than 100 miles away from home (with the exception of about a dozen countries). This coverage also extends to spouses and unmarried dependent children.

• You are covered for $2,500 of medical expenses for such occurrences with only a $50 deductible per person.

• If hospitalization is expected to last eight days or longer, and you are traveling with dependent children, MasterAssist will arrange and pay for their safe return home.

• If you are traveling alone and will be hospitalized outside the U.S. for more than eight days, MasterAssist staff can arrange and pay for an economy class round-trip ticket to bring one relative or friend to your bedside.

• In the event of the death of an immediate relative while traveling outside the 50 United States, they will arrange and pay for a cardholder's return trip to the U.S.

• In the unfortunate event of the death of a cardmember or covered family while traveling, MasterAssist will make all necessary arrangements and pay for shipment home of the remains of the deceased.

● **Emergency translation services**

  (VG, GMC, MCBC, AX, DC)

  Provide free telephone translation services and will help secure a local interpreter at your expense if more assistance is needed.

● **Lost luggage coverage**

  (American Express and Diners Club)

  • With Diners Club you are covered for $1,250 above and beyond the carrier's indemnity. This coverage is based on *replacement* value of items.

  • With American Express Platinum you are covered for up to $1,250 for carry-on baggage and up to $500 over and above the coverage provided by the common carrier for checked baggage. Many of the American Express Corporate cards also include this lost luggage insurance coverage. With the normal American Express card you are covered for reimbursement up to $200 for delayed bags and up to $500 in excess of the airline's liability if your checked or carry-on bags are lost or damaged. You can also purchase additional lost baggage insurance. American Express coverage is for *original* cost.

● **Valuable document delivery**

  If you forget a critical document, the cardmember assistance center can arrange to pick up and deliver the document to you.

● **Frequent flyer mileage**

  Many credit cards now give frequent flyer mileage, based on your overall spending. Nearly every airline has a Visa or MasterCard affinity card, which gives you mileage with them, so you'll have to decide which airline you want to collect mileage on, and apply for that affinity card. The amount of mileage you can get is usually subject to a monthly limit. Most frequent flyer affinity cards include CDW coverage. But as of late 1997, Continental, TWA, Midwest Express, Southwest and United's standard cards did not include this.

American Express *Membership Miles (1998 program)* according to their Web site, offers mileage points on five U.S. airlines (Delta, Continental, TWA, Southwest and Hawaiian) and seven foreign airlines, plus seven hotel chains and Hertz car rentals. Cardmembers pay an extra fee with most of their cards for this program. The program can be linked between different American Express and Optima accounts.

Diners Club *Club Rewards* program offers mileage on practically every major airline, awards with virtually every rental car company and most hotel companies, with no extra fee, and no expiration dates. Diners Club also sends catalogs with hundreds of gift and office items which may be redeemed for mileage. Mileage may be transferred to any participating program. It is by far the best of the credit card frequent flyer deals.

● **Airport lounge usage**

(Diners Club and American Express Platinum)

This often overlooked benefit is a real moneysaver for international travelers. Diners Club has a network of more than 50 clubs at clubs throughout the world. Virtually every club is in Europe, Asia or South America. The network keeps growing. Cardmembers can get access no matter what airline they are flying.

The American Express Platinum card is linked with Continental and Northwest airport clubs. Only cardholders flying on Continental, Northwest or KLM can use these clubs.

Author's credit card recommendations

These recommendations are based strictly on the travel benefits offered by the cards.

☆ Choose **DINERS CLUB** if you are a frequent traveler for either business or pleasure.

- Their CDW insurance is the best—primary, full coverage either domestic or international for up to 29 days.

- Club Rewards is the best credit card frequent flyer mileage program.

- The baggage insurance is based on replacement costs (limited to $1,250).

- The common carrier life insurance is the best available with credit cards and covers free travel such as frequent flyer travel.

- The network of international airport lounges that may be used by Diners Club members is one of the best offered with the fewest restrictions.

- The LeCard dining discount program is a secret bonus that provides 20 percent discounts at select restaurants in major cities across the U.S.

☆ Choose **MASTERCARD BUSINESSCARD** for its medical coverage. These benefits far surpass anything offered by other cards.

Tax rights

One class of rights nearly all travelers have, but don't know much about, concerns taxes, notably sales taxes here in the United States and Value Added Taxes (VATs) in many other countries.

The pleasant fact is that in the U.S. you may not have to pay sales taxes if you ship purchases to your home state, and when traveling in foreign countries with VATs, you can often have the taxes reimbursed when you leave the country.

✔ These tax avoidance actions can save you as much as 24 percent on some purchases in Europe, 7 to 19 percent in Canada, and up to 8.5 percent here in the United States.

United States

In the U.S. when making a large purchase in a state with a hefty sales tax (one greater than the sales tax in your home state), you may ask the store to ship the item to your home. This way you can avoid sales taxes altogether, or at least be charged the lower tax rate of the state to which the merchandise has been sent. This procedure can also help trim your luggage weight but let you enjoy all your souvenirs when you get home.

Canada

In Canada, there is a national Goods and Services Tax (GST), similar to VAT, of 7 percent. Plus, in nine out of 10 Canadian provinces an additional Provincial Sales Tax (PST) levied.

Refunds of GST can be claimed for taxes paid on items taken out of Canada within 60 days of purchase.

You can also get GST refunds for hotel rooms. The list of items which do *not* allow GST refunds includes gasoline, tobacco, alcoholic beverages, meals, car rentals and camping fees.

To file for a refund of GST you must fill out GST refund forms available in most hotels and many stores. These forms are then returned to Canada with *originals* of all receipts upon which you are requesting credit. The minimum refund is Cdn$7 and if your claim is less than Cdn$500 a day you may make your claim at the border. In any case all claims must be made within one year of any purchase involved in the claim.

NOTE: The minimum purchase to qualify for a GST/ PST refund is Cdn$50. This is a per receipt minimum which means three receipts of Cdn$20 apiece will not qualify for a tax refund. Tax refunds are limited to one refund process per calendar year quarter.

This is not a speedy process. At the border or airport, expect at least 15 minutes of paperwork even if you have all your *original* receipts together. It is not difficult to calculate the time required based on observation of the people in line in front of you.

NOTE: If you process your GST claims by mail, the government will return your receipts with your refund. If you are also claiming a refund for PST taxes, send the request in after you complete the GST portion of the refund—the provinces do not normally return the receipts.

Canadian Tax-Free Shopping is an organization that will take care of the paperwork to get your GST and PST taxes refunded.

Contact them at the following address or at the Web site noted below. They will send you a kit to process your tax refunds or you may download most forms from the Internet site.

Canada Tax-free Shopping Inc.
33 Laird Dr.
Toronto, ON
Canada M4G 3S9
Internet Address: http://taxfree.ca/

F-1 Refund Services Inc.
Box 2645, Banff, Alberta
Canada. T0L 0C0
http://www.f1gst.com/

Canadian Provincial Sales Taxes

Canada has 10 provinces and two territories. Nine of 10 provinces impose provincial retail sales tax on goods and certain services that are either produced and/or manufactured in, or imported into, the province.

Each province has its own retail Sales Tax Act and regulation, administrative practices and policies. The tax rate also varies between provinces from 5–12 percent. Goods shipped from one province to another are subject to tax in the province in which they are used.

■ **PST refunds** are not permitted on meals or automobile rentals. Refunds must be requested from each province separately and each has a different procedure for requesting them. The refund forms may be obtained at many stores, hotels and visitor centers. As with GST, PST refunds require receipts with taxes clearly noted, and proof that the items have been exported, but the PST refund request must be received in the provincial offices within 30 days of the purchase. Here, a GST/PST refund service can really help. Otherwise is will be difficult to get both sets of taxes refunded within the governmental refund timelines.

Europe

Value Added Taxes (VAT) in Europe are a way of life. Virtually everything you purchase, from a *Wurst* or *café* on the street to the latest fashions in trendy boutiques, has VAT included somewhere. It should always be clearly marked on your bill or receipt if you ask for one.

These VATs are not chicken feed. They run up to 24 percent in some countries, and vary depending on what you purchase—luxury goods are saddled with a higher tax than necessities.

Theoretically, anyone taking any goods out of a country could be reimbursed the VAT paid on items purchased there, but it was much easier to explain and legislate the theory than it is to actually accomplish tax refunds.

VAT refund counters at airports will stamp receipts, approve refund claim forms and provide envelopes to send VAT refund claims back to the stores from which items were purchased. However, these systems are slow, slow, slow. In addition, you'll have to return forms to *each* store in which you made purchases.

Value added tax refunds require minimum purchases. These minimums range from none in Ireland to highs of around US$210 in France and about US$340 in Switzerland and Liechtenstein. Other sample minimums in local currency are: Germany—DM50, Sweden—SKr200, Italy—Lire300,000, Spain—Pts.15,000, and U.K.—£30.

Maximum VATs in Europe
(as of January 1, 1998)

Austria	16.7%
Belgium	17.4%
Croatia	13.0%
Denmark	20.0%
Finland	18.0%
France	17.1%
Germany	13.0%
Greece	15.3%
Hungary	20.0%
Iceland	19.7%
Italy	20.0%
Ireland	17.4%
Liechtenstein	6.5%
Luxembourg	13.0%
Netherlands	14.9%
Norway	18.7%
Portugal	14.5%
Slovenia	24.2%
Spain	13.8%
Sweden	20.0%
Switzerland	6.1%
Turkey	23.0%
U.K.	14.9%

VAT refund programs

A simplified VAT refund program in Europe includes at least the countries listed in the table above. This program is called Europe Tax-free Shopping (ETS) and organizers expect it to continue to expand. Basically, ETS does all the paperwork for you for a 20 percent commission. Here's how it works:

- Look for a store displaying the ETS shopping logo. Over 100,000 stores and boutiques, and Europe's largest department stores, participate.

- When you make your purchase, ask the salesperson to fill out a VAT-refund check. This refund check reflects the VAT you paid, with the 20 percent service charge deducted. When you leave the country, you get the check stamped by customs officials and then cash it at one of 3,000 windows at most airports and several border crossings. Some of these windows will even convert your funds to U.S. dollars, and others will transfer credit to your credit card.

- For information on this system write:

  European Tax-Free Shopping
  707 Summer Street
  Stamford, CT 06901

  Tel. 800-566-9828 or 203-965-5145;
  fax: 203-965-5481

  Internet address:
  http://www.taxfree.se/index0.html

There are other VAT refund services, but no others with the network of airport kiosks and such individual customer service. The American Express Corporate card also has a VAT refund service with a group called Meridian VAT Reclaim based in Dublin, Ireland (http://www.meridian-vat.co.uk/index.htm).

Consular Services

What can they do for you?

There are two sections of consular services from which Americans traveling abroad may need assistance—the Passport Office and the Citizen Services Office.

The Passport Office handles the issuing of new passports (see next page). The Citizen Services Office handles about everything else. Rather than solving problems, they attempt to provide travelers with enough information to help themselves.

◆ They maintain lists of English-speaking lawyers and doctors. They may know one specializing in your problem or illness.

◆ U.S. officials are usually notified within 48 hours if you are arrested. They will visit, explain the justice system, check on conditions, and help contact your family.

◆ Consulates can quickly transfer emergency funds through the Citizen Services Trust Fund. However, they do not in general pay expenses or lend money.

> ✔ **NOTE:** The consulate or embassy is not a bank—it can't cash checks or make loans; it is not a travel agency—it can't make hotel reservations or flight arrangements, or recommend sights.

What to do if your passport is lost

✔ About 27,000 U.S. passports are lost or stolen abroad every year.

❏ Report the loss immediately to local authorities.

❏ Contact the closest U.S. embassy or consulate. There is always a duty officer on call who can usually get you a replacement or obtain permission for you to return to the States.

❏ If you have lost all your identification, bring along anyone who can vouch for your citizenship, or anything that might prove your identity (plane tickets, engraved jewelry, a prescription bottle, or the like).

❏ Do not go to the airport and expect to be allowed to board a plane back to the United States. This won't work and you're wasting precious time.

❏ Make two copies of all travel documents and identification papers before you leave—e.g., tickets, driver's license, passport. Take one copy (keep it separate from your passport) and leave one with someone back home whom you can call in an emergency.

❏ If you find your passport after you've already applied for a new one, return the old one to the passport-issuing office.

❏ If you received a limited/emergency passport abroad, upon arrival home, take it to a passport agency with proof of citizenship, identification and explanation of loss. They will issue a new permanent passport.

---

from *Travel Holiday*, compiled with assistance from the U.S. State Department

EFFECTIVE
COMPLAINING

When passengers comment on airline service, most airlines do listen. They analyze and keep track of the complaints and compliments they receive and use the information to determine what the public wants and to identify problem areas that need special attention. They also try to resolve individual complaints.

Like other businesses, airlines have a lot of discretion in how they respond to problems. Within your legal rights, your demands for monetary compensation will probably be subject to negotiation, and the kind of action you get depends in large part on the way you go about complaining.

Start with the airline. Before you call or write the DOT or some other agency for help with an air travel problem, you should give the airline a chance to resolve it. Uncle Sam usually doesn't get involved in consumer disputes that go beyond luggage, overbooking, delays and cancellations on domestic flights.

Consumer Reports Travel Letter notes a phenomenon called Merkel's Law (supposedly named after a veteran ticket agent): *A passenger no longer standing in front of you is no longer a problem.* Daily, this law comes into play unless you push the customer service representative into a corner. Ask if an on-the-spot rule waiver might solve the problem.

As a rule, airlines have troubleshooters at the airports (they're usually called Customer Service Representatives) who can take care of most problems on the spot. They can do a lot to immediately make your problems easier to deal with.

They can:

- arrange meals and hotel rooms for stranded passengers
- write checks for denied boarding compensation
- endorse tickets to other carriers
- arrange for luggage repairs
- send delayed luggage to your home
- provide taxi vouchers to hotels or between airports
- provide meal and drink vouchers
- settle other routine claims or complaints that involve relatively small amounts of money.

If you can't resolve the problem at the airport and want to file a complaint, it's best to call or write the airline's consumer or customer relations office. Take notes at the time the incident occurs and jot down the names of the airline employees with whom you dealt. Keep all your travel documents (ticket receipts, baggage check stubs, boarding passes, etc.) as well as receipts for any out-of-pocket expenses that were incurred as a result of the mishandling. Here are some helpful letter-writing tips.

- Type the letter and, if at all possible, limit it to one page.
- Include a daytime telephone number where you can be reached.
- No matter how angry you may be, keep your letter businesslike in tone and don't exaggerate what happened. If the complaint sounds very vehement or sarcastic when you read it back, you might consider waiting a day and rewriting it.

- Start by saying what reservations you held, what happened and at which ticket office, airport or flight the incident occurred.

- Send copies, never the originals, of tickets, receipts or other documents that can back up your claim.

- Include the names of any employees who were rude or made things worse, as well as especially helpful employees.

- Don't clutter up your complaint with petty gripes that can obscure what you're really angry about.

- Let the airline know if you've suffered any special inconvenience or monetary loss.

- Say just what you expect the carrier to do to make amends. An airline may offer to settle your claim with a check or some other kind of compensation, possibly free transportation. You may only want a written apology from a rude employee—but the airline needs to know what you want before it can decide what action to take.

- Be reasonable. If your demands are way out of line, your letter could earn you a polite apology and a place in the airline's crank files.

If you follow these guidelines, the airlines will probably treat your complaint seriously. Your letter will help them to determine what caused your problem, as well as to suggest actions the company can take to prevent the same thing from happening to other travelers.

Contacting the Department of Transportation and FAA

If you want to put your complaint about an airline on record with the DOT, call the Aviation Consumer Protection Division at 202-366-2220 and leave a recorded message or write:

Aviation Consumer Protection Division
U.S. Department of Transportation
C-75 Room 4107
Washington, D.C. 20590

The Consumer Protection Division will not return calls, but will review all calls, add them to their complaint database, go over all letters carefully and forward them on to the appropriate airline official for action.

Letters from consumers help the DOT spot problem areas and trends in the airline industry. Every month they publish a report with information about the number of complaints they receive about each airline and what problems people are having. They also use DOT complaint files to document the need for changes in the DOT's consumer protection regulations.

Whether you call or write, please be brief and concise in the description of your problem and be sure to include the following information: your name, address and daytime phone number including area code, the name of the airline or company about which you are complaining, the flight date, flight number, and origin and destination cities of your trip.

If you write, you should also include a copy of your airline ticket (not the original) and any correspondence you have already exchanged with the company.

The DOT also has a section of their Web site (http://www.dot.gov/ost/ogc/index.html) devoted to costomer service questions. It includes DOT publications and fact sheets as well as airline reports.

If your complaint is about a safety hazard, call or write to the Federal Aviation Administration:

Community & Consumer Liaison Division
APA-200
Federal Aviation Administration
800 Independence Avenue, S.W.
Washington, D.C. 20591

Toll-free: 800-FAA-SURE

Office hours: Monday - Friday
8 a.m. to 4 p.m. Eastern Standard Time

Safety issues include carry-on baggage, child safety seats, airport security procedures, aircraft malfunctions, air traffic systems, and hazardous materials.

The U.S. Government Printing Office offers books and pamphlets covering many of your travel rights including *Fly Rights,* which is incorporated in this book, *Child/Infant Safety Seats Recommended for Use in Aircraft*, and *Your Trip Abroad*. Write for the free Consumer Information Catalog, P.O. Box 100, Pueblo, CO 81002.

Small Claims Court

All consumer problems can ultimately be taken to Small Claims Court if passengers feel they have not received just compensation for problems.

DOT has a section of their Web site that outlines procedures (http://www.dot.gov/ost/ogc/subject/consumer/aviation/publications/telljudge.html).

Travel industry consumer protection programs

These two organizations provide good industry-based consumer affairs programs:

American Society of Travel Agents (ASTA)
1101 King Street
Alexandria, VA 22314
Telephone: 703-739-2782

United States Tour Operator Association
211 E. 51st Street, #12B
New York, NY 10022
Telephone: 212-944-5727

ASTA may be able to help if your complaint is against a member travel agent or one of the travel suppliers booked *through* a travel agency. You must submit complaints to ASTA within six months of the incident.

The United States Tour Operator Association represents about 40 large wholesale tour operators. Their assistance programs are very helpful when member organizations are involved.

Local consumer help programs

In most communities there are consumer help groups that try to mediate complaints about businesses, including airlines and travel agencies.

 Most state governments have a special office that investigates consumer problems and complaints. Sometimes it is a separate division in the governor's or state attorney general's office. Check your telephone book under the state government listing.

- Many cities and counties have consumer affairs departments that handle complaints. Often you can register your complaint and get information over the phone or in person.

- Your local Better Business Bureau can often help resolve disputes.

- A number of newspapers and radio or TV stations operate Hot Lines or Action Lines where individual consumers can get help. Consumer reporters, with the help of volunteers, try to mediate complaints and may report the results as a news item. The possible publicity encourages companies to take fast action on consumer problems when they are referred by the media. Some Action Lines, however, may not be able to handle every complaint they receive. They often select the most severe problems or those that are most representative of the kinds of complaints they get.

- *Condé Nast TRAVELER* has sections called Ombudsman and Question & Answer that provide help in settling some travel-related problems. However, their problem solving and answers are limited to those problems they discuss in the magazine. The address and fax numbers for these sections are published monthly in the magazine, or contact them through their Web site (see page 148).

- A group of radio and TV stations has a "Call for Action" consumer program. If you can't get satisfaction from the travel company, call this hotline at 1-800-647-1756.

U.S. Airline Customer Service Contacts

AirTrans Airways
Consumer Affairs
1600 Phoenix Blvd. #126
Atlanta, GA 30349-5555
☎ 800-825-8538

Air Wisconsin
Consumer Affairs Admin.
W6390 Challenger Drive
Appleton, WI 54915
☎ 920-739-5123 ext. 4217

Alaska Airlines
Dir. Consumer Affairs
PO Box 68900
Seattle, WA 98168
☎ 206-431-7286

Aloha Airlines
Mgr. Customer Relations
PO Box 30028
Honolulu, HI 96820
☎ 808-836-4115

America West Airlines
Mgr. Customer Relations
4000 E. Sky Harbor Blvd.
Phoenix, AZ 85034
☎ 602-693-6019

American Airlines
Dir. Consumer Relations
PO Box 619612 M/D 2400
Dallas/Ft. Worth Airport
Ft. Worth, TX 75261
☎ 817-963-1234
or 817-967-2000

American Trans Air
Consumer Affairs
PO Box 51609,
Indianapolis Intl. Airport
Indianapolis, IN 46251
☎ 317-243-4140
or 800-225-2995

Continental Airlines
Customer Care
3663 Sam Houston Parkway,
E. #500
Houston, TX 77032
☎ 800-932-2732

Delta Airlines, Inc.
Dir. Consumer Affairs
Hartsfield-Atlanta Airport
PO Box 20980
Atlanta, GA 30320-2980
☎ 404-715-1450
fax: 404-715-1495

Hawaiian Airlines
Mgr. Consumer Affairs
PO Box 30008
Honolulu, HI 96820
☎ 808-835-3424

Horizon Air
Mgr. Customer Relations
PO Box 48309
Seattle, WA 98148
☎ 800-523-1223 ext. 601

Kiwi Int'l Airlines
Hemisphere Center
6th Floor
Newark, NJ 07114-0006
☎ 973-645-1133

Midway Airlines
Consumer Relations
300 W. Morgan St. #1200
Durham, NC 27701
☎ 800-564-5001

Midwest Express Airlines, Inc.
Consumer Affairs Specialist
4744 S. Howel Avenue
Oak Creek, WI 53154
☎ 414-570-4000

Northwest Airlines
Dir. Customer Relations
Dept. C-6590
5101 Northwest Drive
St. Paul, MN 55111-3034
☎ 612-726-2046

Reno Air Customer Service
PO Box 30059
Reno, NV 89520-3059
☎ 702-954-5000
fax: 702-858-4957

Southwest Airlines
Dir. Customer Relations
PO Box 36647
Love Field
Dallas, TX 75235-1647
☎ 214-792-4223

Tower Air, Inc.
Mgr. Customer Service
Hangar No. 17
JFK Int'l Airport
Jamaica, NY 11430
☎ 718-553-3598 or 553-4610

Trans World Airlines (TWA)
Staff VP Customer Relations
1415 Olive Street #100
St. Louis, MO 63103
☎ 314-589-3600

United Airlines
Dir. Customer Relations
WHQPW
PO Box 66100
Chicago, IL 60666
☎ 874-700-2214

USAirways
Dir. Consumer Affairs
PO Box 1501
4001 N. Liberty Street
Winston-Salem, NC 27102
☎ 910-661-0061

Westair Airlines
Customer Service
5580 Air Corp. Way
Fresno, CA 93727
☎ 209-294-6915

International Airlines Customer Service Offices

Aer Lingus
Customer Service
538 Broadhollow Road
Melville NY 11747
☎ 516-577-5704

Air Canada
Air Canada Center
Zip 233
PO Box 14000
Station Airport Dorval
Quebec
H4Y 1H4 Canada
☎ 800-813-9237

Air France
Customer Relations
125 W. 55th Street
New York, NY 10019
☎ 800-872-3224

Alitalia Airlines
Customer Relations
666 5th Avenue
New York, NY 10103
☎ 800-903-9991
fax: 212-903-3507

Austrian Airlines
Customer Service
17-20 Whitestone Expwy
Whitestone, NY 11357
☎ 718-670-8612
fax: 718-670-8619

British Airways
Customer Service
75-20 Astoria Blvd.
Jackson Heights, NY 11370
☎ 800-545-7644
fax: 718-397-4395

Canadian Airlines Int'l.
Calgary Admin. Bldg.
Customer Relations
615-18 Street S.E.
Calgary, Alberta,
T3E 6J5 Canada
☎ 403-569-4180

Cathay Pacific Airways
Customer Relations
590 5th Ave. 5th floor
New York, NY 10036
☎ 888-888-0120 ext. 112
fax: 212-944-6519

El Al Israel Airlines
Public Relations
120 W. 45th Street
New York, NY 10036
☎ 212-852-0634 baggage
or 212-852-0611 other

Finnair
228 E. 45th Street, 8th Floor
New York, NY 10017-3303
☎ 212-499-9000
fax: 212-499-9040

beria Airlines
Customer Relations
100 Blue Lagoon Dr. #200
Miami, FL 33126
☎ 305-262-9612
ax: 305-262-0594

celandair
Customer Relations
950 Symphony Woods Rd.
Columbia, MD 21044
☎ 410-715-1600
ax: 410-715-3547

orea Airlines
101 W. Imperial Highway
os Angeles, CA 90045
☎ 310-417-5200
ax: 310-417-3051

ufthansa German Airlines
ustomer Relations
540 Hempstead Turnpike
ast Meadow, NY 11554
☎ 516-296-9650
x: 516-296-9660

Iexicana Airlines
ustomer Service
341 Airport Blvd. #200
os Angeles, CA 90045
☎ 800-353-8245
x: 310-646-0433

antas Airways
ustomer Relations
1 Apollo St. #400
Segundo, CA 90245-4741
310-726-1407
x: 310-727-1401

SAS Scandinavian Airlines
Customer Relations
9 Polito Avenue
Lyndhurst, NJ 07071
☎ 800-345-9684
fax: 201-896-3735

Singapore Airlines
Public Affairs
5670 Wilshire Blvd.#1800
Los Angeles, CA 90036
☎ 213-934-8833 ext.132 & 325
fax: 213-939-6727

Swissair
Customer Service
41 Pinelawn Road
Melville, NY 11747
(complaints by letter only)

Thai Airways International
22 N. Supulveda Blvd.
El Segundo, CA 90245
☎ 310-640-0097 ext 274/5
fax: 310-640-8202

Virgin Atlantic Airways
Customer Relations
747 Belden Avenue
Norwalk, CT 06850
☎ 800-496-6661
fax: 203-750-6420

Car rental customer service contacts

Avis
Customer Service
900 Old Country Rd.
Garden City, NY 11530
☎ 800-352-7900 or
516-222-4200

Alamo
Customer Relations
PO Box 22776
Ft. Lauderdale, FL   33335
☎ 800-445-5664

AutoEurope
Customer Relations
39 Commercial Street
Portland, ME 04112
☎ 800-223-5555 or
207-842-2000
fax: 207-842-2222

Budget
Customer Relations
PO Box 111520
Carrollton, TX 75011
☎ 800-621-2844

Dollar
Consumer Services
100 N. Sepulveda Blvd.,
6th Floor
El Segundo, CA 90245
☎ 800-800-5252

Hertz
Customer Relations
PO Box 26120
Oklahoma City, OK 73126
☎ 800-654-4173
fax: 800-645-9925

National
VP, Customer Service &
Quality
7700 France Ave. S.
Minneapolis, MN 55435
☎ 800-367-6767
or 612-830-2951

Thrifty
Customer Service
PO Box 35250
Tulsa, OK 74135
☎ 800-334-1705

Value
Customer Service
PO Box 5040
Boca Raton, FL 33431
☎800-327-6459

Credit card contacts

American Express
Green ☎ 800-528-4800
Gold ☎ 800-327-2177
Platinum ☎ 800-525-3355

Diners Club
☎ 800-2-DINERS

Discover Card
☎ 800-DISCOVER

Visa & MasterCard: These have different benefits and customer service contacts depending on the issuing bank—call the phone number on the back of your card.

Appendix:
Pet rights

Over two million pets and other live animals are transported by air every year in the United States. Federal and state governments impose restrictions on transporting live animals. In addition, each airline establishes its own company policy for the proper handling of the animals they transport. As a shipper or owner you also have a responsibility to take the necessary precautions to ensure the well-being of the animal you ship.

Because each airline establishes its own policy, it is important to check with the air carrier you intend to use. However, the following are some of the provisions you will probably encounter at most airlines.

Airlines generally require health certificates from all shippers. So it's a good idea to have a licensed veterinarian examine animals within 10 days prior to shipment and issue a certificate stating that the animal is in good health.

The following is from *Plane Talk*, written by the U.S. Department of Transportation.

The **Animal and Plant Health Inspection Service of the U.S. Department of Agriculture enforces the Federal Animal Welfare Act**. Here are several of the more important requirements.

- Dogs and cats must be at least eight weeks old and must have been weaned for at least five days.

- Cages and other containers must meet the minimum standard for size, ventilation, strength, sanitation and design for safe handling. (Sky kennels furnished by the airlines meet these requirements.)

● Dogs and cats must not be brought to the airline for shipping more than four hours before departure. (Six hours is permitted if shipping arrangements are made in advance.)

● If puppies or kittens less than 16 weeks of age are in transit more than 12 hours, food and water must be provided. Older animals must have food at least every 24 hours and water at least every 12 hours. Written instructions for food and water must accompany all animals shipped, regardless of the scheduled time in transit.

● Animals may not be exposed to temperatures less than 45 degrees Fahrenheit unless they are accompanied by a certificate signed by a veterinarian stating that they are acclimated to lower temperatures.

● Animals cannot be shipped COD unless the shipper guarantees the return freight should the animals be refused at destination.

Transporting pets as baggage

A pet may be transported as baggage if accompanied on the same flight to the same destination. Some air carriers may impose a special fee or excess baggage charge for this service. Pets may be shipped as cargo if unaccompanied, and many airline cargo departments employ specialists in the movement of animals. Animals must always be shipped in pressurized holds. Some airlines allow the kennel to be carried in the passenger cabin as carry-on luggage if it fits under the seat.

In addition to compliance with federal regulations and airline company policy, there are a number of precautions the owner/shipper can take to ensure the welfare of a shipped pet.

- Before traveling, accustom your pet to the kennel in which it will be shipped.

- Do not give your pet solid food in the six hours prior to the flight, although a moderate amount of water and a walk before and after the flight are advised.

- Be sure to reserve a space for your pet in advance, and inquire about time and location for drop-off and pick-up.

- Try to schedule a nonstop flight; avoid connections and the heavy travel of a holiday or weekend flight.

- Inquire about any special health requirements such as quarantine for overseas travel (including Hawaii).

- Be sure to put your name and the recipient's name, address and phone number in large letters on the kennel.

✔ With careful planning, your pet will arrive safely at its destination.

Pet shipping problems

You may want to think twice about shipping your pet as baggage. Recent reports indicate that despite all the regulations, the pets are having a rather hard time in very hot weather.

News stories have revealed shocking cases of pet handling problems—56 puppies died on a TWA flight; 32 dogs died on Delta flights; 24 dogs passed away on United Airlines flights; and five dogs died on American Airlines. The Humane Society of America has received complaints about every major airline in the country.

Court cases have held that a pet that dies during a flight, even if by extreme cold or extreme heat under the airline's control, is, *leagally speaking*, nothing more than a piece of checked baggage. Pets are subject to the same lost/damaged baggage rules that dictate the monetary damages to be paid on your old suitcase (see pages 61-69). As the American Airlines spokesman so delicately puts it, "an animal is checked baggage from a legal liability standpoint."

Pet rights vs. passenger rights

Most of these regulations serve to allow transportation of pets. What happens when a passenger is allergic to a pet that has been brought aboard as hand baggage? This happened to a passenger recently traveling on a full flight. She learned that the pet's right to fly was more important than her right to breathe comfortably. Her only alternatives were to exchange her seat with a non-allergic passenger or to deplane (without compensation) and catch a later flight.

If the pet has been properly booked on the flight as carry-on baggage, it can fly and is treated with the same rights as its owner.

The moral of the story: If you have an allergic reaction to animals, let the reservationist know, or if you see a pet being carried aboard speak immediately with the gate personnel so they can maneuver to find you a seat out of harm's way.

Index